Exploring
ISSUES
of
LIFE

Exploring......
ISSUES
of
LIFE

Brian D. Johnston

HAYES PRESS
Leicester

First published by Hayes Press 1994

Unless otherwise indicated, biblical quotations are from the
New International Version.

ISBN 1 871126 14 2

British Library Cataloguing-in-Publication Data.
A catalogue record for this book is available
from the British Library.

Production and Printing in England for
Hayes Press, Essex Road, Leicester, LE4 7EE by
Nuprint Ltd, Station Road, Harpenden, Herts AL5 4SE

CONTENTS

FOREWORD

'Keep your heart with all diligence, for out of it spring the issues of life' (Proverbs 4:23, NKJV).

This book aims to explore biblical attitudes to some of today's issues. God says in Isaiah 55:8 : *'...my thoughts are not your thoughts'*, so we need to be prepared to have our thinking adjusted from that of society around us, and be willing to swim against the flow. Paul writes in Romans 12:2: *'Do not conform any longer to the pattern of this world, but be transformed by the renewing of your mind.'* In this context 'world' means the society around us in terms of its beliefs, values and lifestyle. The views of our peers in society exert a considerable pressure on us. This is graphically described in J.B. Phillips' paraphrase of the above verse: 'Don't let the world around you squeeze you into its own mould, but let God re-mould your minds from within'. There's great pressure to conform; it's not easy to be different. This matter of being different is spoken of in terms of 'transformation'. We are to be 'transformed disciples'. This word pictures for us a caterpillar-to-butterfly type change. It's the same word that's used to describe the change when Jesus was 'transfigured' on the mountain (Mat. 17). Disciples ought to be like their Lord. How we wish we were more like Him and less like the world around us in our attitudes!

How can this be realised in our lives? By the renewing of our minds. By letting the whole attitude of our minds be changed. Again, we say 'how'? How can we have a renewed mind? Surely only by habitually meditating on the Word of God by the Spirit's help; until the principles of God's Word become absorbed into our thinking, and such thinking governs all our actions. On the issues that face us today, we long that we might be able to say with Paul: *'. . . we have the mind of Christ'* (1 Cor. 2:16). That is, that we might come to treat such issues in a truly Christian way, from a distinctively Christian point of view.

It is my hope that the material presented in this book might be of some help in looking at things in this way. All Bible quotations are from the New International Version unless otherwise indicated. The material contained in the various sections has been selected on the basis of the criterion that this is intended as a 'should we?', and not a 'how to' type of book. It's hoped that the main Bible references in the section headings, the short discussion that follows, together with the study questions at the end of each section, will form the basis for fruitful discussion groups. To this end, the study questions, and also a summary of the key sub-issues, will enable the reader to develop the issues individually or in groups. The key sub-issues may be enlarged and photocopied or used for overhead projection.

In our quest, this book is only a beginning.

INTRODUCTION

The Bible speaks of some people who '... *understood the times*' (1 Chron. 12:32). We, too, need to understand the times in which we live if we are to avoid absorbing 'the spirit of the age', and following its trends. First of all, we need to be aware of what is happening, and who is masterminding it (Eph. 2:2).

Dazzling scientific and technological progress in this space-age has gone hand in hand with a decrease in the 'fear of the Lord'. Advances in branches of science, such as medicine, pose increasing ethical dilemmas.

Moral values of previous years are now regarded as out-dated and irrelevant in our increasingly corrupt society. The divine institutions of marriage and the family are coming more and more under attack in these days of the so-called 'new morality'. The accent today is on 'fulfilment', 'enrichment' and 'broad-mindedness', as seen, for example, in 'open marriages'—where either partner is 'free' to engage in sexual relations outside of the marriage. Many do not even bother with marriage at all. Anything goes in the pursuit of pleasure and gratification, sometimes with the proviso that no-one gets hurt. However, the sad reality is that many, including children, are physically or emotionally scarred for life. Society's morals are no longer Bible-based, even when the establishment promotes responsible-sounding 'safe' sex policies. As a result, the media and entertainment world has become increasingly explicit, as well as sophisticated, in its coverage of topics. Today's advanced visual technology provides us with challenges unprecedented in former times. Powerful advertising and media messages bombard us, and attempt—all too successfully—to shape our thinking, by projecting 'images' for us to conform to. These are often poles away from the biblical message that we should be seen to be *in His (God's) image*. It's so easy for us to adopt the latest definitions of 'acceptable' and 'successful' and 'necessary'.

Greed and the drive for gratification give rise to a society where law and order become more difficult to maintain, and where sex and violence are brazenly glamorised.

In the religious sphere, pseudo-Christian cults and occultic influences, often with a message that takes us back to the original deceit, continue to emerge and suggest the political and economic landscapes of tomorrow.

The Psalmist might well say in Psalm 11:3: *'When the foundations are being destroyed, what can the righteous do?'* Foundational values in society around us are crumbling today. Today's Christian, however, will still find a firm foundation in God's Word. In this connection, we can say: *'... God's solid foundation stands firm'* (2 Tim. 2:19).

The Bible, accepted as being with full authority, is the believer's anchor against today's fast-flowing current of change. Human fashions change and are short-lived like *'... the flowers of the field'*, but God's Word is, by contrast, eternal (see Isaiah 40:6-8). In it we find timeless principles which remain vitally relevant. Our defence against the erosion of our beliefs and values is by absorbing these principles into our thinking. This advice is not new, of course. Psalm 119:9-11 says: *'How can a young man (or woman) keep his way pure? By living according to your word. I seek you with all my heart…I have hidden your word in my heart that I might not sin against you.'*

So, Christian believers who want God's best for them will allow themselves to be guided by God's Word, but how do we, practically, hide God's Word in our heart? We ought not to study the Bible as we would a text-book, or rule-book. We need prayerfully to cultivate our relationship with the Lord around our open Bible. Times we spend with our Bible, our Quiet Times, are to be times of fellowship with the Lord. In this way it's no mere duty, far less a drudgery—it's a thrill as we get to know better the Person we love! In our daily Quiet Times we should:

1) Make sure we are fully awake and alert.

2) Pray, asking God to help us concentrate and understand what we read.

3) Read through our planned Bible portion for the day (not too long). It's helpful to follow a systematic programme of readings.

4) Think over what we have read. If it's a story, try to imagine it happening as though we were there. A suitable daily reader guide can be very helpful to get us started each day, but we must be sure to think for ourselves as well. In any case, we should pay attention to the meaning, context and application of the passage.

5) Make a note of any promises, warnings, commands etc. We can especially note anything we have read which we can specifically relate to the Lord.

6) Pray, turning the themes of our reading into themes for thanksgivings, requests, etc. We can ask for further help in specific difficulties we may have come across in our reading. We should also thank the Lord for anything we feel He has clearly shown us, for example about our lifestyle or about Himself.

7) Begin to apply it in our life.

By such an habitual procedure we renew our minds in His presence. As we enjoy the Lord in the Word, we will readily give expression to Christian principles we find there to guide us. By remaining in the Lord Jesus (John 15), we will draw all our resources from Him through close fellowship. Having our hearts open to His love, we will want to express it to others. One aspect of that will be our desire to fulfil His command to witness. Our greatest aim will be to become more like our Lord (Phil. 3).

In all these ways we will be helped to keep in step with the Spirit of Jesus, and not the spirit of the age we live in.

GLOBAL
ISSUES

1.1 THE ENVIRONMENT

—does it matter how 'green' we are?

Main Bible Reading: Genesis 1:26-31

'Then God said, "Let us make man in our image, in our likeness, and let them rule over the fish of the sea and the birds of the air, over the livestock, over all the earth, and over all the creatures that move along the ground."

So God created man in his own image, in the image of God he created him; male and female he created them.

God blessed them and said to them, "Be fruitful and increase in number; fill the earth and subdue it. Rule over the fish of the sea and the birds of the air and over every living creature that moves on the ground."

Then God said, "I give you every seed-bearing plant on the face of the whole earth and every tree that has fruit with seed in it. They will be yours for food. And to all the beasts of the earth and all the birds of the air and all the creatures that move on the ground—everything that has the breath of life in it—I give every green plant for food." And it was so.

God saw all that he had made, and it was very good. And there was evening, and there was morning—the sixth day.'

What are we to make of all the fuss about 'ozone-friendly' and 'CFC-free'? For many years now it's been fashionable to be 'green', as mankind has wakened up to some of the damage being done to planet earth. How important should this issue be to us? Is there a distinctly Christian perspective?

Whose earth is it anyway?

Recently I met with other trustees of our local church hall to consider our responsibilities this year in caring for the fabric of the building. The property doesn't belong to me, but since I was appointed as one of the trustees, I've been entrusted with helping to ensure that it remains in good serviceable condition. It's something like this with regard to the planet. It doesn't belong to us, for we read *'The earth is the LORD's'* (Ps. 24:1). It belongs to God because He made it. After He made it, He didn't just abandon it, He sustains it (Heb. 1:3). He is no 'absentee landlord'. The 'laws of nature' express His will. *'In him we live and move and have our being'* (Acts 17:28). He did, however, delegate authority over the planet to mankind in the beginning: *'So God created man in his own image... God blessed them and said to them, "Be fruitful...; fill the earth and subdue it. Rule over the fish of the sea and the birds of the air and over every living creature that moves on the ground... I give you every seed-bearing plant... and every tree that has fruit with seed in it. They will be yours for food"'* (Gen. 1:27-29).

Our creation in God's image meant, among other things, that mankind was given ability to rule and be creative. It's clear from the above verses that we were given a position of delegated authority over the earth. It's in this sense that we can read in Psalm 115:16 *'The highest heavens belong to the LORD, but the earth he has given to man.'* So, God is the owner, but He has given to us a management responsibility. We are His trustees for our environment.

Dominion not exploitation

It's quite appropriate then that we cultivate land, developing tools and technology to help us, especially in a fallen world where such work has become difficult. Furthermore, responsible mining of fuels and minerals; damming of rivers and harnessing of atomic energy are not necessarily illicit ways of exercising our God-given dominion to provide for our needs.

However, the first chapter of Genesis was not a blank cheque to men and women to do as they pleased. It provided for management, and not mismanagement of resources; and for meeting our need, but not our greed. The command to 'subdue' was not one to destroy or exploit our environment. Today the planet suffers from disproportionate pollution, and use of resources, by 'the North' (North America, Europe and Japan) on the one hand, and the unsustainable methods of development by 'the South' (Asia, Africa and Latin America) on the other. Each 'hemisphere' defends its own practices on economic grounds, and criticises the other's on ecological grounds.

The complexity of the issues

Whether by encountering rubbish scattered over a hill-side during a country walk, or by seeing a documentary on deforestation or desertification, we are constantly made aware of the problems facing the planet today. However, the causes giving rise to the problems are often complex. For example, the environmental evils of deforestation, such as soil erosion with consequential famine and even climate change, are linked to the need for developing countries to support export trade and service vast national debts.

Desertification—the loss of vegetation cover and deterioration of the soil—is another major problem that threatens productive land throughout the world. This environmental catastrophe is a major contributor to famine in Africa. More than a quarter of the world's land surface is affected by desertification, and shows how we mismanage earth's resouces. It's right for us to be grieved at the extent to which mankind has fallen short of the early command to *'Be fruitful and...fill the earth'*.

Keeping it in perspective

Clearly then, biblical convictions regarding creation and stewardship should make us environmentally concerned. However, Christians cannot identify with all of the motivation of environmental pressure groups. Beware, too, of the hi-jacking of environmental concerns by the New Age philosophy (with its worship of 'Mother Earth'). Our concern stems primarily from the acknowledgement that the earth is the LORD's (not ours), and also our desire to obey and please God (not self-preservation). The issue is not of top priority for a Christian, as distinct from expressing our love for God and for fellow human-beings, which is to be preeminent among our concerns. We must not allow ourselves to be deflected from the principal goals of our discipleship (Mat. 28:18-20; Phil. 3:7-21).

Some practical steps
Nevertheless, we can express our concern in the following ways:

—by reading e.g. Psalm 148 and praying to share God's concern
—by caring for our own locality, e.g. removing eyesores
—by wasting as little as possible
—by recycling whenever we can
—by switching to lead-free petrol where appropriate
—by replacing only when necessary, avoiding consumerism
—by buying 'environmentally friendly' goods when available
—by buying brands known not to exploit 'Third World' workers
—by taking bags with us when shopping to avoid packaging
—by considering the options of buying second-hand, or sharing
—by giving to the poor for sustainable development projects
—by writing to local authorities suggesting better recycling facilities, public transport and so on.

As Christians we wait for the coming of the Lord, and a time when the desert will bloom again, as this groaning creation is liberated (Rom. 8:21). And then, He will make all things new (Rev. 21:5).

▽   FURTHER STUDY QUESTIONS   ▽

- What do the land sabbaths (Lev. 25:1-7) teach us of God's care for the environment?

- How does your attitude to the environment around you need to change?

- When did you last praise our Creator God for His handiwork seen in creation?

- Is Isaiah 24:5 applicable to this issue?

- Have you balanced this matter correctly with the direct claims of discipleship?

SUMMARY

FOR GROUP STUDY

THE ENVIRONMENT

* Whose earth is it?

* Biblical convictions: creation and stewardship

* Dominion not irresponsible exploitation

* The complexity of the issues

* Practical steps

* Keeping it in perspective

1.2 MILITARY INVOLVEMENT
—a question of war or peace

Main Bible Reading: Romans 12:17—13:7

'Do not repay anyone evil for evil. Be careful to do what is right in the eyes of everybody. If it is possible, as far as it depends on you, live at peace with everyone. Do not take revenge, my friends, but leave room for God's wrath, for it is written: "It is mine to avenge; I will repay," says the Lord. On the contrary:

> *"If your enemy is hungry, feed him; if he is thirsty, give him something to drink. In doing this, you will heap burning coals on his head."*

Do not be overcome by evil, but overcome evil with good.

Everyone must submit himself to the governing authorities, for there is no authority except that which God has established. The authorities that exist have been established by God. Consequently, he who rebels against the authority is rebelling against what God has instituted, and those who do so will bring judgment on themselves. For rulers hold no terror for those who do right, but for those who do wrong. Do you want to be free from fear of the one in authority? Then do what is right and he will commend you. For he is God's servant to do you good. But if you do wrong, be afraid, for he does not bear the sword for nothing. He is God's servant, an angel of wrath to bring punishment on the wrongdoer. Therefore, it is necessary to submit to the authorities, not only because of possible punishment but also because of conscience.

This is also why you pay taxes, for the authorities are God's servants, who give their full time to governing. Give everyone what you owe him: If you owe taxes, pay taxes; if revenue, then revenue; if respect, then respect; if honour, then honour.'

An instant after the megaton nuclear warhead exploded, a huge fireball, three quarters of a mile across, burst upwards. At its centre the temperature was estimated at more than eight times the heat at the centre of the sun. Blast effects generated scorching winds and waves of suffocating heat. Glass and metal melted. Steel, concrete, buildings, roads, bridges, and hundreds of thousands of people were vapourised. Up to four miles from the centre of the blast everyone was killed. The raging cauldron sucked everything up into a towering 25 mile high mushroom-shaped cloud.

This description is based on Hiroshima and nuclear bomb test data, and vividly portrays a power for devastation that is present in our world.

The facts alone are awesome. No other period of history has witnessed warfare on the scale of this century. Wars have dominated the twentieth century, with well over 200 having taken place. International military spending has exceeded that which goes on education, health and foreign aid.

Historically, Christians have not agreed on their attitude to war and whether it could ever be morally acceptable to participate. Broadly, there are two views.

There are those who would not rule out involvement in war where it could be viewed as the lesser of two evils, a painful necessity in a fallen world. In such a view it is necessary to decide when a war is justified. This condition is considered met if a war is thought to have a just cause, and to discriminate between combatants and non-combatants. It should also have a reasonable expectation of achieving the desired result. Romans 13:1-7 is interpreted as saying that the Christian, when acting as an agent of the state, can legitimately use violent means to resist evil. This principle is then extended to international affairs. Old Testament examples of wars are quoted in support of this 'Just War' point of view. Since war was right, at times, for God's people in the past, so, it is argued, it cannot always be unacceptable for a believer to get involved today.

The other main view is 'Pacifism'. Here it is recognised that God's people were rightly involved in warfare in the past, and that in the future the Lord Himself will wage war. War is, therefore, not regarded as always intrinsically evil but, in this context, the pacifist believes he is bound without exception by the teaching of the Sermon on the Mount, precluding any armed resisting of evil. It is not, however, the Christian's business to condemn the government should it decide to embark on war. This is the type of thinking that led many believers to stand as 'conscientious objectors' during, for example, two world wars.

The basic question is: *'Can it ever be right for a Christian to "...bear the sword"'* (Rom. 13:4)? This seems to go against the tenor of the Sermon on the Mount, as well as Romans 12:14, 17-21. Some settle for making a difference between acting personally, or on behalf of the State (the latter being viewed as *'...God's servant'*—Rom. 13:4). But can we really make such a division? Is it always going to be possible to do this? In extreme cases, someone acting for the State cannot ignore his own personal moral responsibility. Early in 1992, a former East German border guard was convicted of the manslaughter of a man shot while attempting to flee to the West. He was sentenced to three and a half years in prison—specifically, the trial judge said, for following the laws of his country rather than asserting his conscience. The court evidently could not distinguish between 'person' and 'office'. Now, bearing in mind the teaching of the Bible, could a believer on the Lord Jesus ever be justified in taking life, even if this was sanctioned by the State? The answer is surely no.

In trying to resolve the tension we've been considering, are we not on safer ground simply to say that the State has been given a role by God which has been expressly forbidden for the Christian to participate in personally? If the State declares war, the Christian is to submit (Rom. 13:1), and so not to protest against such a course of action, but that subjection cannot be to the point of personal involvement (Compare the case of Acts 5:29). At the same time, the Christian does well to show due sensitivity to the issue of his benefitting from the sacrifice, even of life itself, made by others who serve in the armed forces.

Someone, however, may object to this use of the command: *'Do not resist an evil person'* (Mat. 5:39). We must certainly guard against taking it too literally, and outside of its context, as defined in the four illustrations the Lord went on to give in His famous Sermon. Whereas the Law, in saying an eye for an eye, limited retaliation to an equivalent measure; Jesus' teaching seems to be demanding that His disciples forego the right to revenge so completely as to be prepared to accept double the insult or injury instead. But does this need to mean absolutely no self-defence is allowed, for example if we're mugged? Surely, in such cases the spirit of non-retaliation wouldn't be breached by warding off an attacker. However, defending a country against another aggressor nation is totally different. It would inevitably involve inflicting casualties. We're not comparing like with like; the tension remains, and so the point made above stands. Furthermore, is it thinkable that members of the Body of Christ should ever put themselves in the position of taking the life of a fellow-member?

There are, of course, other verses that help us. In John 18:36, the Lord spoke of His disciples as not fighting because *'My kingdom is not of this world.'* We are also described as being *'...in the world'* but *'...not of the world'* in John 17:11 and 16. It follows that we should not seek to impede God's sovereign purposes being worked out in a fallen world.

The Lord expects us to be peacemakers (Mat. 5:9), following after peace with all men (Heb. 12:14) in this world, which will increasingly be characterised by war until Jesus returns (Mat. 24:6). Then He will bring about peace. There is '... *a time for war and a time for peace*' (Eccles. 3:8).

In line with 1 Timothy 2:1,2, of course, our main duty is to voice our concern to God in prayer. Prayer is a more effective deterrent that any threat of force could ever be.

▽ FURTHER STUDY QUESTIONS ▽

- What are the objections against ever going to war in this era, and what do you think of them?

- Why didn't John the Baptist command the soldiers to resign their post (Luke 3:14)?

- How far would you take the non-retaliation command of the Sermon on the Mount?

SUMMARY

FOR GROUP STUDY

MILITARY INVOLVEMENT

* Just war versus Pacifism

* Romans 13:4 versus Romans 12:14

* Other considerations, principally John 18:36

* The deterrent of prayer

1.3 POLITICS
—how do you vote on this one?

Main Bible Reading: Romans 13:1-7

'Everyone must submit himself to the governing authorities, for there is no authority except that which God has established. The authorities that exist have been established by God. Consequently, he who rebels against the authority is rebelling against what God has instituted, and those who do so will bring judgment on themselves. For rulers hold no terror for those who do right, but for those who do wrong. Do you want to be free from fear of the one in authority? Then do what is right and he will commend you. For he is God's servant to do you good. But if you do wrong, be afraid, for he does not bear the sword for nothing. He is God's servant, an angel of wrath to bring punishment on the wrongdoer. Therefore, it is necessary to submit to the authorities, not only because of possible punishment but also because of conscience.

This is also why you pay taxes, for the authorities are God's servants, who give their full time to governing. Give everyone what you owe him: If you owe taxes, pay taxes; if revenue, then revenue; if respect, then respect; if honour, then honour.'

Additional Readings: 1 Peter 1:6,7; 2:13-19;
1 Timothy 2:1,2

How far, if at all, should the Christian get involved either in expressing political opinions, or engaging in political activities? In the context of democracy, isn't voting a requirement of our submission? Don't we have a moral duty to protest against non-Christian practices? How, otherwise, can we truly be the 'salt of the earth'?

The disciple of the Lord Jesus will be willing to be guided by the teaching of the Bible on such matters. Romans 13 is very much to the point. Before we moan about the Government and its politicians, let's stop and recognise that God has put them there! That's the reason—and not whether we agree with them or not—why we're to be subject to the governing authorities, regardless of their political colour. So, when an unpopular, or discredited tax is levied, there's to be no question of us not paying (see also Mat. 22:21).

Romans 13:1,3 isn't referring only to the principle of government, but specifically to its personalities, '... *the governing authorities*' and '... *rulers*'. Not that their rise to power necessarily carries with it God's seal of approval, for the sovereign God at times raises up even '... *the lowest of men*' (Dan. 4:17 RV). So, we must submit to every governing authority, even those whose beliefs and practices are definitely non-Christian (even though this judgement as to what constitutes non-Christian may be subject to debate among Christians at times!) Even if Christians were to be agreed in opposition to a political party, or rule, then even legal political moves against it would be contrary to the Bible, for, in terms of God's sometimes unfathomable purposes, we might well find ourselves fighting against God.

It's easy to submit when we agree. However, the great Bible principle of submission applies equally when we're in disagreement with the decision reached. When Paul and Peter penned the words in our readings, they were living under an occupying power capable of great cruelty. Peter's readers in the first century had their backs to the wall in the days of Nero, but his message to them by the Spirit of God was not one telling them to protest against injustice, or lobby for a better political scene; rather, his message encouraged them to endure injustice patiently, recognising something of God's sovereign purposes (1 Pet. 1:6,7; 2:13-19). Surely if political action was ever justified it was in their case! But no. The only breaking point to our submission may come if the State compels us to do something very clearly against the specific commands of the Lord, for example if we're commanded not to evangelise (Acts 5:29).

But someone may say: 'Yes, I see that it is God who establishes the government of my land, and that political changes only occur in accordance with His sovereign will. But can He not use the votes and actions of believers, who discern His will, to bring about such changes?' The first thing to say, perhaps, is that God's purposes cannot be thwarted by political campaigns, the ballot-box, or even force of arms. Nebuchadnezzar learnt the lesson: *'No-one can hold back his (God's) hand'* (Dan. 4:35). God's desire is that we should be involved through prayer (1 Tim. 2:1,2) in participating with His will in changing political scenes. *'The king's heart is in the hand of the LORD; he directs it like a watercourse wherever he pleases'* (Prov. 21:1).

The efforts of sincere believers to infiltrate politics with the aim of 'Christianising' society and advancing the cause of evangelism are not supported by the Bible. We follow a Master who, in His earthly example, was never associated with a political party, programme or protest. The reason is found in His declaration before Pilate that His kingdom was '...*not of this world*' (John 18:36). The picture of 2 Timothy 2:3,4 is quite uncompromising: '*Endure hardship with us like a good soldier of Christ Jesus. No-one serving as a soldier gets involved in civilian affairs—he wants to please his commanding officer.*' This world is a battlefield. We're on the front-lines, engaged in a spiritual conflict against the spiritual forces of evil (Eph. 6:12). We must not allow ourselves to be deflected by secular affairs. How tragic when we hear national religious figures today ever ready to offer political advice, but with no spiritual message. The fact is that the commitment to a government implied by voting, is really incompatible with the Christian's resignation of the affairs of government to divine control; especially when account is taken of the extensive liberties governments take with basic issues of integrity and honesty.

The same applies largely to trade union involvement; something which the Christian does well to minimise. A leadership role in this field, or even participation in 'industrial action' (e.g. strikes), cannot escape the borderland of political activity and insubordination to '...*the powers that be*' (Rom. 13:1 RV). A whole range of other fringe political initiatives, including e.g. national referenda, political lobbying, and some kinds of petitioning, draw the disciple of Christ into associations and part commitments to a variety of movements which have no empathy with his or her primary commitment to the Lord. At the same time, disciples may from time to time feel compelled to register a protest or appeal to governments on issues of public morality, where such intervention would be honouring to God. To do so quite independently of any organisation other than churches of God avoids implied sympathies with other organisations' other objectives.

In pleasing our Commanding Officer, we've got plenty to get on with. We have to love our neighbours, and to do good to all. Our actions are to be geared towards people, not structures; relieving needs, not removing causes; showing compassion, not pushing for reform. Such 'good works' usually result in opportunities to witness. People may then as a result turn to Christ and be brought under God's rule in terms of the order He has set for government among His people within the structure of churches of God. The potential exists there for justice and solutions to problems of need. Then, collectively, we can demonstrate a challenging lifestyle to those outside the Kingdom. Only by being distinct can we exert an influence for good, as we permeate society with the good news of God's rule. Thus, we become '...*salt of the earth*' (Mat. 5:13).

▽ FURTHER STUDY QUESTIONS ▽

- On issues such as proposed changes to religious broadcasting, ought we to write prayerfully to MPs to air Christian views? Backed by prayer, significant concessions have been won in such areas. Is there a difference between electing a government, and seeking to influence whatever government is in power through making representation?

- How do we regard the influence of men like Wilberforce who were instrumental in the abolition of slavery? Did God use individuals as such, regardless of whether or not they were Christians?

- What does the spread of the gospel under hostile regimes (e.g. China) prove as to the benefits we might see in more tolerant regimes?

- In the light of early Christian response to religious oppression in Acts 12, would it be inappropriate to send a written appeal to authorities in lands today where believers are imprisoned for their faith contrary to the constitution?

- In what way was the case of Daniel's involvement different from the above?

- Does John the Baptist's example of speaking out against moral wrongs (although in a time of transition) give any guidance for us today?

- Discuss the relevance of the account of Josiah's meddling as told in 2 Chronicles 35:20-27.

SUMMARY

FOR GROUP STUDY

POLITICS

* Government ordained, not necessarily condoned by God!

* We are to submit to God's sovereignty in this too

* We participate through prayer

* Social action, not reform

1.4 A WORLD OF NEED

—can we afford not to give?

Main Bible Reading: 1 Timothy 6:17-19

> *'Command those who are rich in this present world not to be arrogant nor to put their hope in wealth, which is so uncertain, but to put their hope in God, who richly provides us with everything for our enjoyment. Command them to do good, to be rich in good deeds, and to be generous and willing to share. In this way they will lay up treasure for themselves as a firm foundation for the coming age, so that they may take hold of the life that is truly life.'*

Additional Readings: Galatians 6:10; Isaiah 58; 2 Corinthians 8 and 9; James 2; 1 John 3:17

The depth of need in our world is staggering. Pictures of the emaciated, diseased bodies of children evoke our compassion. The statistics are horrifying:

—800 million people living in poverty
—18 million refugees from their homeland
—30 million displaced within their own land
—at least 1.5 billion still lack basic healthcare and clean water
—40,000 die daily as a result of malnutrition and impure water supplies

— 100 million children will still die from preventable illness and malnutrition during the 1990s
— each night 1 billion people (1 in 5) go hungry to bed
— the North (including Eastern Europe) has 1/4 the world's population and 4/5 the world's income
— the South (including China) has 3/4 the world's population and 1/5 the world's income
— in the South, a child dies of hunger or disease every two seconds

Greed in the North lies behind such figures, although Third World development is also affected by other factors such as:

— mismanagement;
— government extravagance and corruption;
— racism, predjudices and war;
— cultural background.

The needy and the 'down-and-outs' are in our own locality too. In various parts of the world, Christians suffer great hardships. In our own local church some may be struggling quite badly compared to others.

God's concern for the poor and needy comes across throughout the Bible (e.g. see Lev. 23:22 and Gal. 2:10). Sensitive to that today, what should be our Christian attitude and lifestyle?

A careful study of the early chapters of the book of Acts shows that the early Christians did not have a strictly communal lifestyle. They had personal property and possessions which they regarded as a trust from God. They were ready to sell these and make donations to help fellow-believers as needs arose. The letters to the Corinthians, and that by James, show richer and poorer Christians living together in the Christian community. Riches are not condemned in the Bible. Every Christian is not called to go and sell all that he has. What does the Bible say? 1 Timothy 6:17 commands those who are rich not to put their hope in the uncertainty of riches. Rather we're to enjoy God's rich provision for us—however great or small in financial terms. We're definitely warned not to want to be rich (vv 9,10). An attitude of contentment, a simple lifestyle, and a spirit of generosity are urged upon us (vv 6,7,8,18). As we see needs around us we're to be willing to share.

But there's so much need, where are we to begin, and where do we stop? Galatians 6:10 gives us a principle that is also very practical. We are to do good '... *as we have opportunity*'. The good we're to do is to be all-embracing, but a clear principle of priority is given. In its practical outworking, as regards that portion of our giving to the Lord which we wish to use to help needy people, perhaps we can target first of all needy folks in our own church(es), or those within its sphere of influence. We also have a duty to make sure our own families are adequately provided for (1 Tim. 5:8). Then, we can consider needs of other believers around the world as they are known to us. It's important to keep informed. Finally, having met those needs, and again by keeping informed, we can contribute intelligently to help relieve needs all over the world through the schemes of reputable organisations.

Many of the verses suggested for our reading in

this section are primarily in the context of relieving needs among God's people, but, perhaps, they can still be in our minds as we consider the ever-widening circles of responsibility brought before us in our Galatians' verse.

Of course, our giving is something that ought to be directed by a deep prayerful concern, and not simply when our conscience is troubling us. It's too easy to give money then. Such a prayerful concern will also cause us to examine our own lifestyle. Perhaps we should read 1 Timothy chapter 6 again. It's so easy to be sucked into a consumerism that exploits the Third World.

▽ FURTHER STUDY QUESTIONS ▽

- What do I consider to be the limits of my responsibility towards those in poverty?

- Would it be wise, or effective, to boycott products of a firm known to be exploiting workers in the Third World?

- How can you help needy people in a way that is not liable to abuse?

SUMMARY

FOR GROUP STUDY

A WORLD of NEED

* There is great need far and near

* God's concern for the poor

* A biblical attitude to riches

* Setting our priorities for giving

SPIRITUAL ISSUES

2.1 THE NEW AGE MOVEMENT
—new truth or old lies?

Main Bible Reading: 2 Timothy 4:3,4

> *'For the time will come when men will not put up with sound doctrine. Instead, to suit their own desires, they will gather around them a great number of teachers to say what their itching ears want to hear. They will turn their ears away from the truth and turn aside to myths.'*

Additional Readings: Genesis 3:4,5

What is the New Age Movement? It cannot simply be described as a new cult. It has no clear leader or structure. It's a loose networking of Western occultism and Eastern religions, which professes to promote world peace and concern for the environment. Disarmament and environmental groups often have strong links with the Movement. It has deeply occultic undertones. Contact with 'spirit beings' is enthusiastically pursued. It's, perhaps, best described as an idea that claims that mankind is close to a breakthrough into a new age, that we are on the verge of evolving a new global consciousness. Its followers believe that the world's economic, military and political problems can only be solved by releasing our own inner human potential.

The basic conviction of this philosophy is the possibility, it is claimed, of discovering our own self-divinity. In denying death, and speaking of 'becoming the god we are', the whole movement is unmasked as having swallowed the original lie of Satan in the Garden of Eden (Gen. 3:4,5): *'You will not surely die... you will be like God.'*

Detecting Satan's hand in all this, we are not surprised at all to discover that some of the following stated goals of the New Age Movement reflect the shape of the end-time prophecies of the Bible:

— One world government
— One world religion
— One world financial system
— A coming world leader (being the expected one of all the world's religions (Lord Maitreya, Hare Krishna, 5th Buddha, Imam Mahdi, Messiah...)

Let's look a little closer at these goals. The Movement's political agenda is one of bringing about a united world government. We hear a lot about a so-called 'new world order'. A golden age free from violence and disease is hailed as being just round the corner. Significantly, although it professes non-racism, the New Age Movement is anti-semitic (hates Jews).

The dominant philosophy of the New Age Movement is Hinduistic. Key elements of belief and practice include: pantheism (all is God), worship of self, the creation and Lucifer, reincarnation and forms of spirit mediumship. God is considered to be an impersonal force, not distinct from creation: the 'aggregate consciousness of all living things'. In their eyes, Jesus was a highly evolved being, and not the Christ (see 2 John 7). The authority of the Bible is rejected, as are any absolute notions of right and wrong. Humanity is considered to share the essential being of God, and so not to be accountable to any higher being. Problems in society and barriers to human evolution (especially in a spiritual sense) are said to be due to our ignorance of personal godhood, resulting in being trapped by bad karma (residual bad effects from evil done in earlier lives). Karma is made the excuse for self-centred and immoral behaviour.

The solution that's presented is by means of a transformation in our thinking. This is described as 'altered states of consciousness', the developing of a unity with all things. Eastern-style meditation, hallucinogenic drugs and spiritism are among the ways of helping to bring about this transformation. The desired outcome is the self-realisation of personal godhood, of being part of 'the cosmic consciousness'. New Agers believe that if enough people achieve this breakthrough then a new age will dawn; that these personal transformations will, in turn, lead to a global transformation. This is the reasoning behind the staging of world meditation rallies with many millions of participants. It is to achieve a spiritual evolutionary quantum leap into divinity and a perfect world where all live as one.

The New Age Movement also foresees a cashless society which permits trading by the initiated only. Compare Revelation 13:7. It's interesting (in view of Rev.13:13-15) that it has devoted a great deal of research into the use of holographic images, even to the point of making claims that 3-D holographic images could now be projected such that they could be viewed by something like a third of the earth's surface at any given time with the sound technology to make the image speak in the languages of the areas being beamed to.

As Christians, we need to discern its 'spirit' (1 John 4:1-3), and be alert to its 'fronts' of relaxing music, some forms of holistic medicine, environmentalism, world peace, etc. New Age ideas are being propagated in films and books, as well as by celebrities. Astrology, the attempt to divine the influence of the stars and planets on human affairs and terrestrial events, a practice forbidden by the Bible (Is. 47), has led many into deeper involvement within the New Age Movement. The business world, too, has been influenced by New Age thinking. Some management training courses aimed at motivation and self-improvement are based on New Age principles. In some cases, education and health professionals ('alternative medicine') are promoting mystical techniques. Transcendental meditation and yoga are increasingly marketed for stress relief and pain management. We do well to bear in mind that yoga is really a form of Hindu prayer. New Agers see it as another means of 'becoming united with the universal soul'. The constituent parts of this Hindu word 'yo' and 'ga', meaning man and god, go right to the root of the New Age heresy. Never has the Lord's command to *'Watch and pray'* (Mat. 26:41) been more necessary.

▽   FURTHER STUDY QUESTIONS   ▽

- What are the key features of a cult?

- What is the verdict of 1 John 4:3?

- Find where spiritism and the occult are forbidden in the Bible.

- What features of 'the falling away' (2 Thes. 2:3 RV) may be discerned in the New Age Movement?

- In what ways have you personally encountered New Age ideas?

SUMMARY

FOR GROUP STUDY

The NEW AGE MOVEMENT

* An occultic philosophy

* The Old Lie reappears

* The shape of things to come:
  One world government, religion and
  finance

* New Age solution:

  — meditation, drugs, spiritism...
  — transformation
  — realise personal godhood
  — evolutionary quantum leap
  — new golden age

2.2 THE ROLE OF WOMEN IN SERVING GOD

—second among equals?

Main Bible Reading: Genesis 1:26-28, 2:18-25

'Then God said, "Let us make man in our image, in our likeness, and let them rule over the fish of the sea and the birds of the air, over the livestock, over all the earth, and over all the creatures that move along the ground."

So God created man in his own image, in the image of God he created him; male and female he created them.

God blessed them and said to them, "Be fruitful and increase in number; fill the earth and subdue it. Rule over the fish of the sea and the birds of the air and over every living creature that moves on the ground."

The LORD God said, "It is not good for the man to be alone. I will make a helper suitable for him."

Now the LORD God had formed out of the ground all the beasts of the field and all the birds of the air. He brought them to the man to see what he would name them; and whatever the man called each living creature, that was its name. So the man gave names to all the livestock, the birds of the air and all the beasts of the field.

But for Adam no suitable helper was found.

So the LORD God caused the man to fall into a deep sleep; and while he was sleeping, he took one of the man's ribs and closed up the place with flesh. Then the LORD God made a woman from the rib he had taken out of the man, and he brought her to the man.

The man said,

> *"This is now bone of my bones and flesh of my flesh; she shall be called 'woman,' for she was taken out of man."*

For this reason a man will leave his father and mother and be united to his wife, and they will become one flesh.

The man and his wife were both naked, and they felt no shame.'

Additional Readings: 1 Corinthians 11:5; 14:34,35; 1 Timothy 2:11-15; 2 Timothy 1:5; Titus 2:4

The glorious fact of the resurrection was first made known to a woman (John 20:10-18). That women should be the first witnesses was quite revolutionary at a time when their testimony wasn't acceptable in a court of law! Other aspects of the revolutionary nature of the way Jesus dealt with women might be seen in that, while some rabbis forbade women to have instruction in the law, the Lord taught Mary while she sat at His feet in the home at Bethany (Luke 10:38-42). One rabbi, Jose ben Johanan, said: 'Talk not much with women'; whereas the Lord held a theologically profound conversation with an immoral Samaritan woman in John 4.

During Jesus' lifetime on earth, there were women who travelled around with the Lord and His disciples '...*helping to support them out of their own means*' (Luke 8:3). Paul, too, later spoke appreciatively of the contribution of female fellow-workers (Rom. 16:1).

Priscilla and Aquila, in Acts 18:26, combined effectively as a husband and wife team to teach Apollos in their home.

All of this, and more, extends the notable contribution of women throughout the Old Testament period. The sacrifice and service of the women who served at the door of the Tent of Meeting is appreciatively recorded. They gave away their mirrors in order to adorn God's house rather than themselves. Such has been the spirit of godly women down the ages. Much more could be said of such women as Deborah (Judg. 4:4), Huldah (2 Kin. 22:14), Hannah (1 Sam. 1), Ruth, and others.

So there can be no doubt, then, that women have a role in divine service, although not the same role as men. Let's check out a few principles:

1. In God's Image: Men and women were both created by God, and given joint responsibility (Gen.1:27,28) as being equally '*in the image of God*'.

2. The Order of Creation: Man, nevertheless, was created first, and the Bible gives weight to this order (1 Tim. 2:13) as establishing a preeminent authority relationship: '...*the head of the woman is man*' (1 Cor. 11:3). Woman was made from man (Gen.

2:18); however, the word for 'helper' (Hebrew: ezer) is never used in the Bible of an inferior.

3. The Consequences of the Fall: As a result of the first woman being deceived, her lot was confirmed as being one of subjection to her husband; and the bearing of children was to become the means through which she would be 'saved', or preserved, in her God-appointed role (Gen. 3:16; 1 Tim. 2:14).

4. Gifted as Members of the Body: All believers are members of the Church which is called Christ's Body (Mat. 16:18; Eph. 1:23). In this there is no distinction between male and female (Gal. 3:28). It is as members of the Body that we are gifted by God (Rom. 12; 1 Cor. 12; Eph. 4). So, women too have gifts, to be used in an appropriate way in the context of the service of churches of God.

5. Interdependence in Service: In the New Testament setting of churches of God, the interdependence of men and women is recognised (1 Cor. 11:11).

6. Different Roles: Within the New Testament pattern for collective service in churches of God, the roles of men and women are seen to be different, in that men are to lead the church, and women are to acknowledge this by covering their heads and remaining silent (1 Cor. 11:3-16; 14:34,35; 1 Tim. 2:11-15). In each of these instances this is justified by an appeal to Genesis—the order of creation, and the beguiling in the Garden of Eden— and so is not in any way a merely cultural matter subject to change, nor limited to very specific contexts. The general authority relationship laid down at the time of creation (the hierarchy of

Christ—man—woman) is thus specifically applied to the 'in church' situation.

1 Corinthians 11:3-16: This is understood to refer to the church meeting formally 'in church' and to describe women participating as part of a praying or prophesying company, without leading the church in an audible way. This would involve silent prayer, and thoughtfully identifying with the prophet's message. There is then no conflict with 1 Corinthians 14:34,35 or 1 Timothy 2:12. The introduction to this section recalls the hierarchy established in early Genesis. It is as witness to this preeminent authority relationship that the woman's head (her hair being her glory) is to be covered as a token of subjection. All this shows that this was not merely a custom of that period. Different words used in the original make it quite clear that a covering additional to hair is required.

1 Corinthians 14:34,35: The reference to the Law in the requirement for silence here takes us all the way back to Genesis 3:16, and, therefore, makes this a general principle when gathered together formally 'in church'.

1 Timothy 2:12-14: Similarly, this reference to the order of creation and the way the Fall occurred, surely indicates that a general submission on the part of Christian women is in view.

7. *Christ and the Church reflected in Marriage:* In the home (1 Pet. 3:1-5; Eph.5:22), as well as in the church, women are also specifically exhorted to be in subjection. This submission of the wife to her husband is to reflect the headship of Christ over His Church. Many would find such teaching unacceptable today,

but in every case God's instructions are for our benefit. The Lord Jesus Himself is subject to His Father (1 Cor.15:28), and so such a role affords a unique opportunity to show Christlikeness. It's also obvious from this that there's no question of inferiority whatsoever. We remember how the Lord in all His dealings with women showed respect, giving them a dignity which their own culture had previously denied them (e.g. John 4). In fulfilling their role, women, for their part, are entitled to be shown love, respect and consideration. Headship isn't about dominating, but leading by self-sacrifice. Notice that Paul in Ephesians 5:22 says that the submission of wives is '... *as to the Lord*'. As a result, when this is lacking, the basic problem lies in the relationship with the Lord.

The Contribution of Christian Women: The New Testament, however, devotes space to showing what women can do. In those areas within their God-designed role, women will be more effective than men, and their contribution is to be acknowledged and valued. In one of his pastoral letters to Timothy, Paul paints an attractive picture of mature Christian women having the skills and resources to minister to many different groups of people. He writes of them '... *bringing up children, showing hospitality, washing the feet of the saints, helping those in trouble*' (1 Tim. 5:10) as well as devoting themselves to all kinds of good deeds. 2 Timothy 1:5 pays handsome tribute to the influence of a godly mother, shaping the generations to come. Titus 2:4 broadens the scope for the exercise of female expertise to the area of teaching or training younger women in the church. There are, without doubt, areas of need and counselling where female experience is essential. In today's society where, sadly, so many women and children are damaged, the opportunities for caring, female, evangelical contact have perhaps never been so great.

So, let's focus attention on what women can do, rather than on what they are not scripturally permitted to do. Their contribution may not be a prominent one 'in church', but it is a vital one generally in the overall functioning of a local church of God. We need to value more and more the roles of helping, serving, using hospitality and evangelising etc. Our aim should be to ensure that every Christian woman is spiritually fulfilled through discovering, developing and discharging her gift(s).

▽ FURTHER STUDY QUESTIONS ▽

- How can we learn to value the low-profile roles more?

- Is male headship limited to marriage and 'in church' contexts?

- What can we say about the roles of women in public office and business life?

- Discuss the examples of Deborah and Huldah.

- How would you reconcile 1 Corinthians 11:5 with 1 Corinthians 14:34,35?

SUMMARY

FOR GROUP STUDY

THE ROLE OF WOMEN IN SERVING GOD

* Old Testament examples

* The Lord's dealings with women

* Principles from Genesis:
  — in God's image
  — the order of creation
  — 'helper'
  — Genesis 3:16

* Gifted as members of the Body

* Christ and His Church reflected in marriage

* Interdependent in N.T. churches

* Teaching of 1 Corinthians 11,14 and 1 Timothy 2

* The contribution of Christian women

2.3 FASTING

—should we break our feast?

Main Bible Reading: Matthew 6:16-18

> *'When you fast, do not look sombre, as the hypo-crites do, for they disfigure their faces to show men they are fasting. I tell you the truth, they have received their reward in full. But when you fast, put oil on your head and wash your face, so that it will not be obvious to men that you are fasting, but only to your Father, who is unseen; and your Father, who sees what is done in secret, will reward you.'*

Additional Readings: Zechariah 7:5; Matthew 9:15

'Should we fast?' The person asking the question had not been a Christian very long. As a child he had been taught to fast religiously, and now he wanted to know what the Bible taught on the subject.

Let's look at Jesus' teaching on this issue. In Matthew 6:16, in part of what is usually referred to as the 'Sermon on the Mount', Jesus didn't say to His disci-ples: 'You must fast'; He simply said: *'When you fast'*. Then, a little later in the same gospel, in chapter 9 verse 15, when asked about the difference between John's disciples and His disciples on this very issue, Jesus says of His disciples *'...they will fast'* when referring to the time of His absence. So, it seems clear that, although we're not commanded to fast—in the same way that we're commanded to pray, for example— it is, however, the Lord's expectation that His disciples will fast at times.

Throughout the Bible we find examples of individual and group fasting. We'll look at a few now to try to discover some possible reasons for fasting.

* Esther, in Esther 4:16, fasted with others as they prayed earnestly in something of a tight spot;
* In Isaiah 58:4 we read of the desired effect of true fasting being to cause our voice '...*to be heard on high*';
* In the case of Anna (Luke 2:37) we read of worshipping and fasting;
* The church at Antioch (Acts 13:1,2) fasted while seeking the Lord's guidance in an important matter;
* Although it's not explicitly mentioned, perhaps Paul had it in mind in 1 Corinthians 9:27 as one way of buffeting his body to make it his slave, thus gaining the mastery over bodily appetites and cravings.

Biblical fasting always centres on spiritual purposes, unlike hunger striking or health dieting. Above all, God says that it is '...*for me*' (Zech.7:5). We need to guard against ritual or routine fasting that becomes meaningless (see Is. 58).

The timing or duration is not specified for us, but we need to be sensible and informed if we engage in the practice.

▽   FURTHER STUDY QUESTIONS   ▽

- Do we focus more on praying and giving than fasting (see Mat. 6) because some of us may find it easier to do?

- What precautions or preparations are advisable prior to fasting?

- Consider occasions in the Bible when people fasted for short periods, 3 days, or 40 days. What do we learn from this variation of practice?

SUMMARY

FOR GROUP STUDY

FASTING

* An expectation, not a command

* Biblical examples illustrate usefulness
  for:
  —prayer
  —worship
  —guidance
  —overcoming bodily desires

* Not a routine or ritual, but 'for God'

2.4 VEGETARIANISM

—do real Christians eat meat?

Main Bible Reading: 1 Timothy 4:4-5

'For everything God created is good, and nothing is to be rejected if it is received with thanksgiving, because it is consecrated by the word of God and prayer.'

Additional Readings: Leviticus 11; Acts 10; Romans 14

The young man in the market-place seemed very earnest. His head was shaved, and, from his literature as well as from the way in which he was dressed, it seemed as though he was promoting some eastern religion. 'How can you call yourself a Christian if you eat meat?' he asked in exasperation.

Sometimes the question arises within Christian circles—after all, wasn't Adam originally a vegetarian? So, it's worth tackling it from the Bible.

In Genesis 1:29 and 30, we read that God said to Adam: *"I give you every seed-bearing plant on the face of the whole earth and every tree that has fruit with seed in it. They will be yours for food. And to all the beasts of the earth...I give every green plant for food."* It's clear that originally Adam was not intended to kill animals and eat meat. Before Adam sinned in the garden of Eden, animals were not put to death. When sin entered the world, things changed, however. God

Himself killed an animal to provide clothing for Adam and Eve (Gen. 3:21).

Among the Israelites, far from banning meat from their diet, God simply made a difference between what they had to regard as 'clean', and what was 'unclean'. This cleaness was in a ritual, or ceremonial, sense, following the Law of Moses, albeit consistent with good hygiene practice. God said plainly: *"Of all the animals that live on land, these are the ones you may eat"* (Lev. 11:2). No doubt it was this that was in Daniel's mind when, as a captive in Babylon, he *'...resolved not to defile himself with the royal food'* (Dan. 1:8). He couldn't be sure that it was 'clean', so being a conscientious Jew, he abstained.

Today, as the New Testament of our Bibles makes clear, we're not bound to keep the ceremonies of the Old Testament Law. In Mark 7:19, Jesus declared all foods 'clean'. This was the lesson which the Jewish apostle Peter learnt by means of the vision of Acts chapter 10. He saw a large sheet coming down on the earth, containing all kinds of four-footed animals. Then, to his great surprise, he was commanded: *"Get up, Peter. Kill and eat"* (v 13).

Having said this, it is true that there were circumstances where those in the early churches of God were instructed to avoid meat. Some of those who had come to faith from a non-Jewish background, had previously worshipped idols and were used to eating food sacrificed to these idols. While there was nothing wrong with the food itself, Paul writes in 1 Corinthians 8:7 *'Some people are still so accustomed to idols that when they eat such food they think of it as having been sacrificed to an idol, and since their conscience is weak, it is defiled.'* The problem lay in their thinking, not in the food. It would have been very wrong for a believer to eat meat in association with pagan sacrifices which were offered to idols (1 Cor. 10:18-21), for it involved becoming participants with demons. Hence the clear decree to abstain from such practices in Acts 15:29. A believer who didn't have a pagan background, or who was now clear in his own thinking as not having anything to do with ritual sacrifices to idols, did have the liberty to eat any meat. Often meat that had been sacrificed to idols was cheaper to buy, and so seemed a good bargain. Paul sums up in Romans 14: *'One man's faith allows him to eat everything, but another man, whose faith is weak, eats only vegetables...I am fully convinced that no food is unclean in itself. But if anyone regards something as unclean, then for him it is unclean. If your brother is distressed because of what you eat, you are no longer acting in love'* (vv 2,14,15).

So, for us today, we can settle the issue with Paul's words to Timothy (1 Tim. 4:4,5) : *'For everything God created is good, and nothing is to be rejected if it is received with thanksgiving, because it is consecrated by the word of God and prayer.'* And so, remembering to give thanks for it, we are free to enjoy our food!

There are, perhaps, a couple of modern concerns that we should just touch on. One is the use of hormones, antibiotics, growth stimulants, etc. used in the rearing of livestock as part of the meat-production process. Another has to do with the (ill)treatment of animals that are reared for slaughter. Since the Bible does not forbid the rearing and killing of animals for food, we must leave as a matter for our personal conscience any practices that we consider to be unnecessarily cruel to the animals. As for personal health concerns that may arise from the injections and the type of food given to animals during rearing, we should follow the best medical advice we're given. We certainly ought to avoid everything that's unhealthy for our bodies (1 Cor. 6:19,20).

▽ FURTHER STUDY QUESTIONS ▽

- In the light of Acts 15:29, what about eating products that have blood as a main ingredient?

- How far do you take the principle of 1 Corinthians 6 as applying to types of food generally regarded as being unhealthy?

SUMMARY

FOR GROUP STUDY

VEGETARIANISM

* The situation before Adam sinned

* The Law of Moses

* The clear message of Mark 7:19 and Acts 10 for today

* A New Testament concern

* Some modern concerns

2.5 SIGNS AND WONDERS TODAY
—a time of the signs?

Main Bible Reading: Hebrews 2:3-4

> '...how shall we escape if we ignore such a great
> salvation? This salvation, which was first
> announced by the Lord, was confirmed to us by
> those who heard him. God also testified to it by
> signs, wonders and various miracles, and gifts of
> the Holy Spirit distributed according to his will.'

Additional Readings: Acts 2; 1 Corinthians 14

Should we expect to speak in tongues today? After all,
they are biblical, are they not? A young Christian
wrote to me recently asking: 'How can it be correct to
say that some things which were prevalent in apostolic
times (e.g. the gift of tongues) are no longer for today;
while certain other things which took place then (e.g.
believers' baptism) are still definitely for today?' That
is a very good question— how do we distinguish
between what once happened and still ought to take
place; and those things for which it is no longer God's
will that they should continue? In other words: among
those things that are biblical, what is applicable
today?

Three important questions:

In coming to an understanding of any part of the Bible, we need to ask ourselves: 'What does it mean? What is its context? How does it apply to me?' By the time we understand what we are looking at, and have got it in perspective, then we are already a long way towards applying it. At that point three choices face us: namely to apply it either in practice, or in principle; or, indeed, not to apply it at all.

The case of Acts 2:41,42

'Those who accepted his message were baptised, and about three thousand were added to their number that day. They devoted themselves to the apostles' teaching and to the fellowship, to the breaking of bread and to prayer.'

These familiar words provide a good standard. In relation to those early converts, we are familiar with the steps of salvation, baptism and obedience, the latter expressed in addition to the Church of God at Jerusalem. Is this merely descriptive, or also prescriptive? In other words, do we have the choice to do something different? In using the framework suggested above, we understand the words to mean being made free from condemnation, then being dipped in water in identification with the Lord Jesus as Leader (and symbolising a clear separation from their past life), and then subsequently submitting to the Lord's teaching for disciples in collective Christian service. It's impossible to ignore the Bible-wide context taking us back to the Exodus story which features: the rescue from slavery; the passage through the Red Sea (see 1

Cor. 10:2); and then the commitment to obey the Word of God at Mt Sinai. In the epistles there is also further corroboration that these fundamental truths are applicable to every age. So we understand them to be prescribed for our practice today.

The issue:

However, in the same chapter of Acts we read of the phenomenon of speaking in tongues. Should this also be applied today? Can we pick and choose what we wish to apply? No, we must return to our framework of meaning, context, and application.

What is meant by 'tongues':

First, let us examine what was meant by this phenomenon. The New Testament records tongues as occurring in four locations, namely Jerusalem, Caesarea, Ephesus and Corinth. The words used in Acts 2:4,6 to describe speaking in tongues strongly support the view that ordinary languages were spoken. These were understood by the multinational gathering in Acts 2, but required interpretation to those unfamiliar with the languages in the Corinthian church setting. That the tongues-speaker was personally edified is clear from 1 Corinthians 14:4, yet Paul spoke of his understanding being *'unfruitful'* (v 14: presumably in that it didn't convey anything to his hearers). We conclude the thoughts being expressed were understood by the speaker, rather than the words themselves (else interpretation would seem to be unnecessary). Despite their association with multilingual centres, there is no evidence from which to infer that tongues normally had a missionary purpose in overcoming foreign language barriers. Indeed, 1 Corinthians 14:2 states categorically that the speaking was '...not...to men but to God'. This was exactly the situation in Acts 2:11 when they were speaking the mighty works of God. The tongues phenomenon had attracted the attention of the unbelieving, but the communication of the gospel from verse 14 was delivered by Peter in the ordinary language of the Diaspora.

The context of 'tongues':

Secondly, what of their context? Bible-wide, short periods of miraculous gifts are noted in the days of Moses and Joshua, as well as in the time of Elijah and Elisha. These punctuated long periods of time when human agency was not chosen by God for miraculous activity. When spiritual service was restored in the days of Ezra and Nehemiah there was no hint of a miraculous ministry. Old Testament indications, however, were given of the coming miraculous period of the Lord and the apostles. Peter, at Pentecost, quoted Joel's prophecy. More interesting is the reference to Isaiah 28 in the context of tongues (1 Cor. 14:21). This would appear to be a typical example of the dual fulfilment of prophecy. Firstly, the Babylonians with their foreign tongue would 'speak to' Israel in judgement, taking them away into captivity. Then, at Corinth, where there was a local Jewish community and trade centre, the New Testament phenomenon of tongues was also seen as a fulfilment of this prophecy. This may indicate that God's primary purpose in the use of tongues was directed towards unbelieving Jews. A survey of Acts tends to support this (think of the proselytes in Acts 2; Peter in Acts 10; and John's disciples in Acts 19). This points to a specific divine purpose at that time. It seems that those of the 'old order' were given this sign to prove that the new revelation was of God. Of the three recorded instances of tongues in Acts, we find in chapter 2 that it is the sign that marks the descent of the Holy Spirit at the beginning of the new era that was then dawning. In chapter 10, it is the sign that marks the further extension to Gentiles in the new era. In chapter 19, it is the sign that marks the further revelation to John's disciples concerning the new era.

About the sign-gifts generally:

Even more significant is the association of the sign-gifts with the apostles. This seems to have been to authenticate their role as resurrection witnesses (cf Ex. 4:1-8) '...*so great salvation...was confirmed [note: past tense] unto us by them that heard; God also bearing witness with them, both by signs and wonders, ...powers and by gifts of the Holy Ghost, according to his own will*' (Heb. 2:3,4 RV). Who were those spokesmen who had been with the Lord? Our answer would certainly have to focus on the apostles. We use the term sign-gift to include tongues, interpretations, healings and miracles. A survey of the New Testament strongly supports their link with the apostles. (See Acts 2:43; Acts 3; 2 Cor. 12:12.) Judging from Acts 9:35,42, the gift of healing wasn't commonplace among Christians even in the time of the apostles.

Incidently, those named as exercising the gift of healing are confined to the apostles along with Philip and Stephen, both of whom were very closely associated with the apostles. Indeed, although others exercised them, there is no proof that the use of these sign-gifts was ever originally initiated independently of the personal ministry of the apostles. Of course, the gift of apostleship has itself ceased, one qualification being that of having seen the Lord (1 Cor. 9:1). Is it not then to be expected that the sign-gifts themselves also ceased within the apostolic period? Ephesians 2:20 speaks of '... *the foundation of the apostles*'. The laying of a foundation is only the initial phase, and to this period the apostles belonged. The foundation, once laid through their teaching, being the commandments of the Lord, is confirmed elsewhere as continuing in force, but the signs which marked the initial time of the laying of the foundation in apostolic days should not be expected to continue. It is the commandments themselves that are important and not certain unsolicited, sovereign manifestations of the Spirit which marked out that time as being new and special.

This view of the sign-gifts having a specific purpose at a special time would tend to be confirmed by the epistles. The pastoral letters give qualifications and warnings only about the use of continuing gifts such as ruling and teaching.

The application:
So, now we must face the question of applicability. Ephesians 2:20 speaks of the churches of God, together forming the house of God on earth, as being

a temple for God in the Spirit (as distinct from the Church the Body). In any view, we must affirm the role of the Holy Spirit. We must be careful not to quench Him, nor grieve Him, as we worship by Him in the unity He provides, in which the elderhood throughout the churches seek to discern what seems good to the Spirit. In our daily lives His fulness and fruit are to be evidenced. We need to be open to the work of the Holy Spirit in our lives, and seek after an experience of God through the Christian disciplines, while developing conformity to Christ in character.

In concluding from the context that the four sign-gifts were bound up with the time-period of the apostles and God's special purpose for them, we are not denying a present role for the other New Testament gifts. Some of these previously had a miraculous expression, but do not require it permanently. For example, gifts of prophecy (which include 'forth-telling'), and words of wisdom and knowledge can be expected to operate today in conjunction with the Word of God. Actually, recorded New Testament 'foretellings' are limited, and, perhaps even then, served mainly to authenticate 'forthtellings'. Since prophets, equally with apostles, belonged to the early foundational period, the revelatory gift of prophecy, in the sense of uttering new authoritative revelation, was also soon to cease. Once the inspired Scriptures were complete and their sufficiency attested to (Jude 3), it would be very wrong for anyone to say: 'Thus says the LORD'. However, we say again that many gifts of the Spirit are still intended to have a continuing role today, and how vital it is that we discern,

SIGNS AND WONDERS TODAY

develop and discharge the gifts we have as members of the Body of Christ.

'Miracles still happen', someone may say, and how thankful we are to see evidences of the presence of a prayer-answering God! Equally, a greater proving of His presence, and of our faith, can come through our being sustained in suffering rather than through experiencing healing.

How does our conclusion of non-applicability, as defined above, square with present reality in terms of the contemporary religious scene? Certain published reviews of modern experience which compare this with the New Testament sign-gifts show a considerable discrepancy. This shows up most clearly in terms of contemporary 'tongues' being characterised as: mainly for private use; a learned technique; and a self-generated, unintelligible utterance unrelated to any known language. When these are taken as being a 'proof' to other believers of some advanced spiritual experience, then this is clearly a denial of 1 Corinthians 14:22. Medical studies today, even by Christian doctors, fail to show anything even remotely approaching the healings in apostolic times. Nowhere does the Bible teach us that present physical healing is in the atonement, or, that our service should be modelled on the special healing ministry of the Lord Jesus. Interviews with leading exponents of signs and wonders have even been known to uncover a basic unsoundness with regard to the gospel itself. While we defend our conclusion in the light of contemporary experience, it is necessary to acknowledge the commitment, fervour and evangelical results in evidence among 'charismatics' today. It is thought-provoking to consider an illustration drawn from Moses' experience of striking the rock, rather than speaking to it as he was told to do (Num.20:8). Water nevertheless flowed showing God's power at work. The blessing that resulted, however, was no authentication that what Moses did was the will of God, for he clearly went against the Word of God.

▽ FURTHER STUDY QUESTIONS ▽

- Are counterfeit miracles possible? (Consider Mat.7:21-23.) Can certain phenomena be self-generated?

- Note the use of 'charisma' in Romans 12, 1 Corinthians 12 and 1 Peter 4:10. Looking at the wide range of type of gift to which this applies, what might the significance of the term be?

- Certain versions of Romans 1, 1 Corinthians 12:1; 14:1,12 mention 'spiritual gifts' where literally it might be translated 'spiritual things'. Discuss which is more appropriate. Is there any justification for special classes of gift?

- Discuss how you might discover, develop and discharge your gift.

SUMMARY

FOR GROUP STUDY

SIGNS AND WONDERS TODAY

* Biblical / Applicable

* 1. Meaning
  2. Context
  3. Application (three choices)
  (ensuring consistent decision-making)
  1. Ordinary language
  2. Primarily to Jews
  3. Apostolic association
  (apostles themselves having ceased)

LIFESTYLE ISSUES

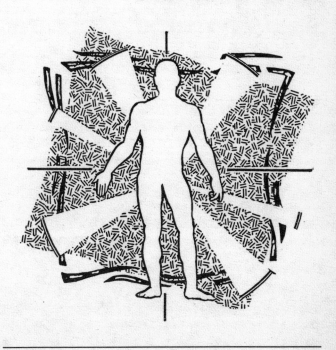

3.1 CAREER AND EDUCATIONAL PLANNING

—making a good job of it

Main Bible Reading: 1 Thessalonians 4:11,12

'Make it your ambition to lead a quiet life, to mind your own business and to work with your hands, just as we told you, so that your daily life may win the respect of outsiders and so that you will not be dependent on anybody.'

Additional Readings: Proverbs 6:6-11; 8:30; 10:4,5; 13:4; 2 Thessalonians 3:6-12

A large group of young Christians had come together to share principles they had applied or learned from others which had guided their approach to education and careers. Questions that they set out to answer included: 'How ambitious should I be?', 'What factors should I rank highest in choosing a job or course?', 'Are there some jobs or careers a Christian should avoid?'

Good questions! Let us try to tackle them from the Bible.

WHY WORK?

1) The God of the Bible is a God who works (Gen. 1:1; John 5:17; Prov. 8:30).

2) Man, even before the Fall, was expected by

God to work. In a fallen world work is often hard. That we should work is therefore one of God's purposes in creation (Gen. 2:15;3:19).

3) God, when giving His Law, legislated for work (and rest) (Ex. 20:9-11).

4) Work teaches us to stand on our own feet (1 Thes. 4:11,12; 2 Thes. 3:6-12).

5) Work is to supply material needs (ours and others) (Prov. 6:6-11; Acts 20:34,35; Eph. 4:28).

6) Work is something we can offer as service to God (Col. 3:17).

Having reminded ourselves that the reason why we work is not just to get rich or gain status, we now go on to consider:

WHAT WORK?
Here we will take a brief look at some factors which have a bearing on our choice:

Aptitude: The first point, surely, as far as our talents and opportunities are concerned, is that we should use our common sense. Parents and children need to be aware of unrealistic expectations, and of the false notion that there is more value in a 'professional' career than in any other. Although that might reflect society's thinking, it is certainly not the Bible's viewpoint. The first Adam was appointed by God as a gardener; the 'Last Adam' (the Lord Jesus, 1 Cor. 15:45) worked on earth as a carpenter.

Money: Money should not be the dominant factor in our choice of employment. We certainly do need to have an income sufficient to provide for ourselves and any dependents (1 Tim. 5:8), but other factors will outweigh this in importance. Our desire should not be to get rich (1 Tim. 6), but to treat money as a resource to be put to proper use.

Time: Obviously, we need to guard against jobs or careers that will take up too much of our time, or the wrong part of our time, so limiting our input to church activities (Heb. 10:25).

Guidance: Proverbs 3:6 is a tremendous promise which we can claim in our career and education planning. Make the decisions before the Lord; after all they are going to affect a large part of your life. The stated condition for God's promise is that we should be acknowledging Him in every area of our lives. That means working through our priorities and putting the demands of a committed disciple lifestyle first (Mat. 6:33). This involves considering...

Location: Avoid being isolated from a church of God. While it is somewhat artificial to consider our career and spiritual life to be in separate compartments, the claims of Christ ought to be paramount over personal advancement. If we are sure that God has both led us to, and is using us in, our local church, let us have the courage to consider declining that glittering promotion if its location is unfavourable in spiritual terms.

Nature: It is important that the type of work we choose will not compromise any of our beliefs or principles. If we, for example, believe it would be wrong for a believer to use violence to combat violence (see 1.2), then clearly there are certain careers in the armed forces and police that would have to be avoided—perhaps any job in those sectors, in view of the 'image' problem. Careers in politics would also be inconsistent with the view taken in the section on politics. Often believers feel that caring professions (e.g. nursing), where compassion can be shown directly, are to be preferred to more acquisitive professions. Remember, however, what was said about aptitude and beware of the down-side of heavy workloads in many such careers. Should we belong to a Trades Union, or is that an expression of an unequal yoke (2 Cor. 6:14)? For some forms of employment being a member will be compulsory. In other cases, we will be guided by our personal conscience as to whether to join, although we certainly would not take part in active, militant action (2 Tim. 2:24).

Evangelism potential: Following the above line of thought, jobs orientated to dealing with people (e.g. teaching, social work) might offer more direct openings to share our faith. Of course, we would have to be sensitive to the appropriate use of our employer's time in the way we go about it. Again, we might like to consider training in skills that have direct applications in mission work (e.g. language, or technical skills used in communicating, or broadcasting). Never underestimate the high pressure demands of certain career or business jobs that can leave us with little reserve in terms of mental or emotional energy for other things. As we have seen, work is something which in itself we can offer as service to God, yet some may wonder if God is calling them to a full-time Christian ministry. This must never be thought of as the ultimate, or ideal, for every believer, although it is God's calling for some. They will have to be sure of the call.

CAREER AND EDUCATIONAL PLANNING

Nehemiah's case is helpful. His call was recognisible in terms of a vision of need, and a personal burden of responsibility to meet that need—a feeling that intensified with time.

HOW WE WORK OR STUDY

Integrity: Our conduct should always be such that we gain the respect of our colleagues or classmates. They will be quick to note if what we are and do does not match what we say. Of course, our expense claims should be 100% accurate. Let us try to follow the uncompromising example of Daniel in Daniel chapter 1. He stuck to the principles with which he had been brought up, when he found himself in a big, foreign city. Compare the case today of being a student away from our usual home environment!

Priority: Matthew 6:33 tells us where our priorities are to lie. As much as the choice lies with us, we could openly decline overtime, or forego extra exam. preparation if, say, it is prayer meeting night. The principle of 1 Samuel 2:30 has many times been proved in situations like this.

Ambition: How ambitious should we be? How keen can we be to get to the top of our profession? How hard should we strive for further education? We will be keen to avoid extremes either way, where our devotion to the Lord, or on the other hand, our testimony, might suffer. We can try to steer a middle course, remembering the secondary importance of our education and career, and the aim of our primary ambition, namely pleasing the Lord (2 Cor. 5:9). We should aim at excellence, more for the sake of our testimony than for purposes of prestige or reward. The disciple's career should be his or her servant, rather than his or her master.

Attitude: From all that we have said, it is clear that we are to work to live, rather that live to work. Our secular employment should be, in greater or lesser degree, supportive of our spiritual service. For some it will, like Paul's tentmaking, be entirely secondary to service for the Lord and '... *whatever you do ... do it all in the name of the Lord Jesus*' (Col. 3:17). After all, how we do something is often more important to God than what we do.

Let's not forget, too, that in times of high unemployment, it can very often be the case, through no fault of our own, that we find that we simply have no job, never mind no choice of job. A friend of mine prefers to say that she's 'in between jobs' rather than unemployed. At least that's a very positive way of coping with what is always a very trying circumstance. We've all seen jovial people transformed into a state of gloominess by sudden, unexpected unemployment. In times of chronic unemployment, years can slip by before alternative employment is found. The endless, tiresome process of applying unsuccessfully for one job after another, and the constant waiting for the postman or a 'phonecall, is wearying and draining to one's morale, self-confidence, and general feelings of usefulness. The challenge to deepen our trust in, and relationship with, the Lord by looking to Him through such a crisis is very real. It never helps to brood, so occupying ourselves purposefully and, above all, praying persistently are vital.

In desperation to find some employment, we may be tempted to compromise on some of the principles outlined above, but God still promises to honour those who honour Him (1 Sam. 2:30).

James writes: *'Consider it pure joy... whenever you face trials of many kinds, because you know that the testing of your faith develops perseverance'* (1:2,3). Sometimes it's only the 'knowing' that God has a purpose that sustains us, and enables us to deepen our dependence on Him. By God's grace we may then be able to say with Paul *'... I have learned to be content whatever the circumstances'* (Phil. 4:11). Paul was content that God knew all his needs and would meet them (Phil. 4:19).

▽ FURTHER STUDY QUESTIONS ▽

- Do you feel there are certain jobs or careers which are best avoided by the Christian? Why?

- Which factors do you rate highest when considering a course, job, or career?

- Discuss the principles which have guided your decisions. What advice would you now give from your own experience?

- How competitive could a Christian be in seeking promotion? What would you do if you felt you had been passed over for promotion?

SUMMARY

FOR GROUP STUDY

CAREER PLANNING

* Aptitude

* Money

* Time

* Guidance

* Location

* Nature

* Evangelism potential

* Integrity

* Priority

* Ambition

* Attitude

3.2 MONEY AND POWER
—at any price?

Main Bible Reading: 1 Timothy 6:6-19; James 2:1-6;
Matthew 5:1-12; Philippians 3:1-16;
Matthew 6:19-24; Mark 10:35-45

Money

'Money makes the world go round', or so the popular saying says. Certainly, society finds inexplicable someone with no desire for money or the possessions and status it can bring. But money can so easily make a fool of us. This is what the Lord pointed out in Luke 12:16-20:

"The ground of a certain rich man produced a good crop. He thought to himself, 'What shall I do? I have no place to store my crops.' Then he said, 'This is what I'll do. I will tear down my barns and build bigger ones, and there will I store all my grain and my goods. And I'll say to myself, 'You have plenty of good things laid up for many years. Take life easy; eat, drink and be merry.'' ' But God said to him, 'You fool! This very night your life will be demanded from you. Then who will get what you have prepared for yourself?' "

Here we can see the hallmarks of a fool. A fool is someone who thinks more of time than eternity; more of their body than their soul and more of their possessions (gifts) than the Giver. In today's materialistic societies, the point made here by Jesus comes home to us with great relevance: life does not consist of material possessions.

We need to face up to this truth in our age when people tend to be defined in terms of their net worth and where there is always the temptation to try to get an even larger piece of the consumer pie, and then to display the trappings of success. 'Money talks', it is said. People jockey to find out what other people earn because in our society money is a symbol of strength, influence and power. Money is used to buy prestige, enlist allegiance and to corrupt people.

As Christians, we need to root out all favoured treatment of people based on money (James 2); human values must be placed above economic ones.

Another strong statement of the Lord Jesus is *'You cannot serve both God and Money'* (Mat. 6:24). As we relate this to purchases, for example, a new house or car, it's challenging to ask ourselves if money or God directs our purchases. Is money our servant or our master?

The New Testament gives examples of the good use of money. The wise men gave of their wealth to the Lord in worship, and we can do the same (Phil. 4:10-20). Zacchaeus, once saved, gave generously, and we're encouraged to do so (1 Tim. 6). Joseph of Arimathea and Nicodemus (John 19:38-42) used their possessions in the service of Christ, as did Barnabas (Acts 4:36,37). We need to use money without serving it. That's not always easy, for money has a seductive character. Surely that's why it's one of Jesus' most frequently recurring themes. Money is referred to in the New Testament in far from neutral terms, for example '...*filthy lucre*', and '*unrighteous mammon*' (1 Tim. 3:3; Luke 16:11 RV). We need to be so careful for it can readily capture our heart. Covetousness is described as idolatry. The '...*love of money*' (1 Tim. 6:10), wanting 'to get rich', and putting our '...*hope in wealth, which is so uncertain*' (1 Tim. 6:17) are identified as problems; not money itself. Although our ambition should not be to become rich, neither are we all called to a life of poverty and the giving away of all our possessions. Rather, we're positively called to a life of contentment, modesty and generosity (1 Tim. 6:6-19).

Strikingly, the Lord tells us that it's better to store up treasure in heaven than here on earth. It's more secure there and draws our affections after it. In practical terms, we can invest in needy lives.

In recent times the so-called 'prosperity gospel' has become hugely popular in some parts of the world. Based on a misunderstanding of verses like 3 John 2, this preaches that God wants all Christians to be rich, and that He'll bless them materially if they do His will. Why this did not apply to the Lord and the apostles is a mystery. God does indeed want us to be rich, but in a spiritual sense however, through His Son who became poor in order that we might become (spiritually) rich (2 Cor. 8:9).

Power
'Power tends to corrupt and absolute power corrupts absolutely'[1], or so the saying tells us. It can so easily

---

[1] J.E.E. Daeberg, First Baron Acton (1904), Letter in Life of *Mandell Creighton* (1), 372.

happen that people in positions of power jockey for position rather than serving the public good. If greed is the downside of money, then pride must be the downside of wielding influence. Anyone with no desire for domination is viewed as strange today.

As we think of the Lord's Sermon on the Mount:
'*Blessed are the poor in spirit, for theirs is the kingdom of heaven.*

Blessed are those who mourn, for they will be comforted.

Blessed are the meek, for they will inherit the earth.

Blessed are those who hunger and thirst for righteousness, for they will be filled.

Blessed are the merciful, for they will be shown mercy.

Blessed are the pure in heart, for they will see God.

Blessed are the peacemakers, for they will be called sons of God.

Blessed are those who are persecuted because of righteousness, for theirs is the kingdom of heaven' (Mat. 5:3-10), we could almost say it turns the world's value system upside down. In contrast to the above, the world's recipe for happiness and satisfaction is to be assertive, not to care who gets trampled on, the end justifying the means, to be competitive, to bend the rules if necessary and to make sure it's only others who get hurt.

The seductive character of power lies in the prestige it offers. We are tempted by fantasies of status and influence and intoxicated with the thought of wielding control over others. The world's way is not God's way. When the Lord addressed those who would be leaders in His spiritual kingdom on earth,

He made clear that their style of leadership was not at all to be modelled on the pattern of secular leadership where people 'lord it over' others. The Lord Himself modelled leadership within the context of service. God-given, delegated authority and Christian subjection must be brought into proper balance.

The apostle Paul talks about 'loss' and 'gain' in relation to his discipleship in Philippians chapter 3. The balance sheet he presents there makes fascinating reading. Previously, he had known 'power' in terms of pedigree, position, and prestige. He now counted these things as 'dung'! The power he now desired was a spiritual power, '... *the power of his resurrection*' (v 10).

Even as the Lord doesn't call us all to poverty, neither do we need to forego all promotion. How much ambition should we have? To become 'top of the heap' should not be high on our list of priorities. Better to make it our aim to pursue excellence and not position; responsibility and not authority. I remember the following advice from a godly Christian who'd been successful in business life : 'If God takes you to the top, and if you can go there with Him—that's fine.'

▽ FURTHER STUDY QUESTIONS ▽

- What lessons in terms of priorities can we learn from Daniel?

- List all the references to money in the teaching of Jesus.

SUMMARY

FOR GROUP STUDY

MONEY

* Wrong values

* The wrong master

* Its seductive character

* Its good use

* The right attitude

POWER

* Wrong values

* Its seductive character

* A better way

3.3 ENTERTAINMENT
—harmless fun?

Main Bible Reading: Philippians 4:8

> *'Finally, brothers, whatever is true, whatever is noble, whatever is right, whatever is pure, whatever is lovely, whatever is admirable—if anything is excellent or praiseworthy—think about such things.'*

Additional Readings: Ecclesiastes 2:1-11; Colossians 3:17

Paul wrote to Timothy of a time when *'People will be... lovers of pleasure rather than lovers of God'* (2 Tim. 3:2,4). How well this describes affluent parts of the world today where many seem to be obsessed with the pursuit of pleasure. The entertainment and leisure industries are big business.

Paul, of course, was not against having a bit of well-earned relaxation—we need that to remain healthy—but he was warning about the obsessive pursuit of pleasure, entertainments and fun that is characteristic of an affluent society today.

Although there is an obvious need for relaxation, recreation and rest in our busy lives, the Christian will want to manage well his or her resouces in this area. In the Old Testament Law, God legislated for rest, following the pattern of His own resting on the seventh day (Gen. 1). Wartime experiments with seven-day working has proved the practical need for a day's rest. The Lord Jesus was careful to suggest a break for His disciples after a period of demanding service. However, devoting time to leisure while failing to obey the command of the Lord about meeting together (Heb. 10:25) is robbing God, as is needlessly spending money on entertainment when the church outreach programme is restricted because of lack of funds. That is our fun at God's expense and is unthinkable for the true disciple!

But are all forms of leisure and entertainment beneficial, or even legitimate, for the Christian wishing to please the Lord?

Certain things are clearly ruled out: *'But among you there must not be even a hint of sexual immorality, or of any kind of impurity, or of greed'* (Eph. 5:3). So, all kinds of pornography which forms the basis of so many films, TV programmes and novels, together with gambling and lotteries in which the motive is acquisitive greed, are ruled out. We need to be rid of anything that hinders our spiritual life (Heb. 12:1). A career in professional sport, for example, would surely distort a Christian's priorities, as well as presenting him, or her, with a whole range of temptations.

While the Bible does not list unacceptable present-day forms of entertainment, it does give timeless principles for us to apply. One of these is found in 1 Corinthians 10:31 where Paul writes: '... *whatever you do, do it all for the glory of God'*. That ought to be a guiding principle when we come to decide exactly what we are at liberty to participate in. We notice, from its context, that this involves consideration for the effect of our actions on others.

The encouragement of Colossians 3:17 is similar: *'And whatever you do... do it all in the name of the Lord Jesus, giving thanks to God the Father through Him.'* So, there is a clear test for us. Can I truly give thanks to God for my participation in this form of recreation? Is it compatible with the honour and authority of His Name. If there is anything 'shady' about what we intend doing, then we would have to reject it on this principle. Consistent with these principles which we have mentioned, sound advice is: 'If you cannot take the Lord Jesus with you, then do not go, or do it, without Him'.

As technology advances, so entertainment becomes ever more sophisticated and accessible. Usually we find each development can have its good and proper use, as well as a bad and harmful one. As we think of the expression *'chambers of imagery'* (Ezek. 8:12 RV), in connection with the power of modern technology to entrance us with its visual images, we must take care not to allow the gradual erosion of God's standards. A Christian who is thoughtful for the things that please the Lord would not, for example, tolerate the glamorisation of illicit sex and gratuitous violence or other corrupt behaviour. In entertainment, leisure and recreation, as with all other areas, God's standards remain uncompromising: *'... whatever is true, whatever is noble, whatever is right, whatever is pure, whatever is lovely, whatever is admirable—if anything is excellent or praiseworthy— think about such things'* (Phil. 4:8).

Having checked that we're not robbing God or doing anything that's ruled out, but rather something that passes the Bible test, let's ensure that we build sufficient recreation into our busy schedules to maintain a healthy balance.

▽ FURTHER STUDY QUESTIONS ▽

- Would professional involvement in sport be wrong for the reason that the 'Entertainment world' is a product of the doomed system of this world, which is opposed to God and alienated from Him?

- Should we only be concerned about the message that any type of music conveys, or is the music style itself part of that message?

- Can you find examples of the good and bad use of music in the Bible?

SUMMARY

FOR GROUP STUDY

ENTERTAINMENT

* healthy relaxation versus obsessive pursuit

* the danger of robbing God

* some forms of entertainment are ruled out

* principles, guidelines, tests and aims

3.4 ADDICTIVE SUBSTANCES
—Christians in a fix?

Main Bible Reading: 1 Corinthians 6:12,19,20

> ' "Everything is permissible for me"—but not everything is beneficial. "Everything is permissible for me"—but I will not be mastered by anything.
>
> Do you not know that your body is a temple of the Holy Spirit, who is in you, whom you have received from God? You are not your own; you were bought at a price. Therefore honour God with your body.'

Additional Readings: Proverbs 23:29-35; Hebrews 12:1-3

By the use of the word 'substance' here we include for our consideration: drugs, solvents, alcohol and tobacco. These do not exhaust the possibilities, but are the main problem areas. By 'addiction' we mean a dependence on any substance which has the capability artificially to alter the mood or feeling of an individual.

There seems to be little scope for disagreement with the view that drug and solvent abuse (e.g. 'glue sniffing') is wrong. Powerful hard drugs such as heroin, cocaine, etc. can cause havoc mentally, morally, emotionally, physically and spiritually among their users. Improper and uncontrolled medical use of drugs (like valium) is also a problem. And, increasingly, soft drugs such as cannabis are available, and fashionable as 'performance enhancers'. Already there is some evidence of possible long term depressive effects from their use. So, quite apart from the question of legality, drug abuse is clearly wrong because of the damage it does to our bodies and minds. The teaching of 1 Corinthians 6:19 is that the believer's body is a temple of the Holy Spirit, and therefore it is to be used for glorifying God and not for abuse by subjecting it to unnecessary dangers.

An interesting United Kingdom statistic shows that more people die as a result of alcohol abuse than die of drug abuse. Alcoholism is the biggest single (drug) addiction problem in western society. The World Health Organisation rates alcoholism as the third largest killer in the western world. Alcohol is the most readily available drug, both in terms of cost and because it is widely available. It is legally sold under licence, and generally socially acceptable in our culture. It is so much a part of modern lifestyle that it is easy to forget that alcohol in sufficient quantity can function as a narcotic substance comparable to illegal hard drugs like heroin. The abuse of alcohol causes problems of huge proportions in society around us. It is a major cause of marital problems, and the destruction of family life. It is a significant factor in many crimes, and accounts for more deaths and injuries through traffic and industrial accidents than anything else. Sensitive to the carnage its abuse causes, believers usually opt for total abstinence, or responsible moderation. The Bible itself warns of the dangers of strong drink (Prov. 23) and condemns drunkenness

(Eph. 5:18; 1 Cor. 6:10). Therefore, it is the misuse of alcohol that must be guarded against. As well as harming our bodies, alcohol taken to excess results in loss of control, so detrimental to the testimony of the believer. By sharp contrast, through being filled with the Holy Spirit, our lives are to be brought under the full control of the Lord the Spirit.

As is the case with alcohol, among believers there are also cultural variations in the strengths of taboos against smoking. Tobacco firms, too, spend vast amounts on advertising in an attempt to lure others into what is for them (the industry) a lucrative habit. The 'worldly' image presented (as in the case of other things too) is not one with which the discerning disciple would wish to identify. Nor would buying cigarettes be a wise way to use our money, since that is a resource entrusted to us by God. Further, there is now also mounting medical evidence linking smoking to the incidence of diseases such as lung cancer, so again, for the sake of safeguarding our bodies which are temples of the Holy Spirit, smoking should be avoided. It could be argued that smoking is no worse than eating unhealthy types of food which are linked to heart complaints. However, as with drug and solvent abuse, there is an even stronger reason for avoidance and that is the power all these substances have to enslave us—to make us servants to bodily appetites. Paul says in 1 Corinthians 6:12: *'I will not be mastered by anything'*. In this respect, smoking is a hindrance to spiritual life and Hebrews 12:1 says: *'... throw off everything that hinders'*.

▽ FURTHER STUDY QUESTIONS ▽

- In connection with 'the social drink', to what dangers should we be alert?

SUMMARY

FOR GROUP STUDY

ADDICTIVE SUBSTANCES

* The health problem

* The testimony problem

* The image problem

* The resource problem

* The addiction problem

PERSONAL ISSUES

4.1 SINGLENESS

—singularly significant?

Main Bible Reading: 1 Corinthians 7:25-38

'Now about virgins: I have no command from the Lord, but I give a judgment as one who by the Lord's mercy is trustworthy. Because of the present crisis, I think that it is good for you to remain as you are. Are you married? Do not seek a divorce. Are you unmarried? Do not look for a wife. But if you do marry, you have not sinned; and if a virgin marries, she has not sinned. But those who marry will face many troubles in this life, and I want to spare you this.

What I mean, brothers, is that the time is short. From now on those who have wives should live as if they had none; those who mourn, as if they did not; those who are happy, as if they were not; those who buy something, as if it were not theirs to keep; those who use the things of the world, as if not engrossed in them. For this world in its present form is passing away.

I would like you to be free from concern. An unmarried man is concerned about the Lord's affairs—how he can please the Lord. But a married man is concerned about the affairs of this world—how he can please his wife—and his interests are divided. An unmarried woman or virgin is concerned about the Lord's affairs: Her aim is to be devoted to the Lord in both body and spirit. But a married woman is concerned about the affairs of this world—how she can please her husband. I am saying this for your own good, not to restrict you, but that you may live in a right way in undivided devotion to the Lord.

If anyone thinks he is acting improperly toward the virgin he is engaged to, and if she is getting on in years and he feels he ought to marry, he should do as he wants. He is not sinning. They should get married. But the man who has settled the matter in his own mind, who is under no compulsion but has control over his own will, and who has made up his mind not to marry the virgin—this man also does the right thing. So then, he who marries the virgin does right, but he who does not marry her does even better.'

Additional Readings: Psalm 68:6; 84:11; 139; Genesis 1; Matthew 19:10-12

People are not like shoes—they don't always come in pairs. Nevertheless, the cultural and social pressures to marry are very real. This pressure is felt by those who've willingly and prayerfully chosen not to marry, as well as by those who may feel that they simply haven't yet had the opportunity to do so.

Peter, a young Christian, had just been best man at his friend's wedding. In front of all the guests, a church friend had nudged his arm and said 'Your turn next, eh?' 'No fear!' Peter had joked without a moment's hesitation, but now that he had a moment to himself he found old insecurities and resentments rising within him.

Why should he be treated as though he was immature, or some sort of second-class citizen simply because he wasn't married? He felt fed up with such insensitive jokes, the pressure he was under from his family to 'settle down', and the impression often given in church that fulfilment was only to be found through marriage. Certain people, no doubt well-intentioned, were forever dropping hints about 'a very nice girl'. Worse were the overheard remarks 'I wonder why he isn't married yet?' or 'He'll have to watch out that he doesn't get left on the shelf!' Wait a minute, was he getting just a little paranoid?

Sue, also, is a single person in her early twenties. She feels that she's sometimes misunderstood, maybe even treated with suspicion. Even so, the fact that some folks in church seem to consider marriage and having a family as the norm, and singleness therefore as somehow abnormal or incomplete, doesn't help her cope with the media's constant message that without an idyllic romantic marriage she's definitely missing out.

Despite reflecting on her past feelings of embarassment, frustration, failure, not to mention a complex about missing out, Sue was thankful for the many true friends she had, of either sex, some of whom were also single, but whose lives were filled with meaning and purpose. One or two of them, she knew, had come to regard their singleness as God's calling for them, while others had later married. After all, it came down in the end to a question of functioning as God intended.

The apostle Paul, in 1 Corinthians 7, doesn't present marriage as a matter of course, but as a decision bound up with the priority matter of our service for the Lord. Neither is it treated as the highest priority in life, but rather that we should grasp every opportunity as individuals for living a full and meaningful life in serving the Lord. Anyone following the teaching of this chapter would avoid having the time to sit around and brood. It's healthy to express emotions, but not to dwell on them. Getting busy helping others is useful, but it's our personal relationship with the Lord Jesus that should be our primary source of fulfilment. Psychologists talk of our three basic needs of security, significance and self-worth. How good it is for us to reflect on the fact that we're loved with a love that we can never lose (security); that we've been personally gifted for a specific role in His service (significance); and that our having been bought with His own blood proves our value in His sight (self-worth).

There are some tremendous promises in the Bible applicable to singleness. For instance, Philippians 4:19: *'And my God will meet all your needs according to his glorious riches in Christ Jesus.'* These words were written by the apostle Paul who appears to have found that his singleness enabled him to deepen his relationship with the Lord. He could say: *'I have learned the secret of being content in any and every situation'* (Phil. 4:12).

We return finally to Peter whom we referred to a moment ago at his friend's wedding. Recognising the fact that God cared for him as an individual, Peter determined again to bring his feelings to God, to accept himself, and to continue to develop friendships with others. He reminded himself of his philosophy: 'I'm single. That's o.k. I'll accept it as being God's will for me at present (Phil. 4:11). Until (and if) He should change my state, I'll get on with the challenge of growing and developing as a person.' Peter relaxed, easier in his own mind now, conscious that while it did not mean that he need do nothing to encourage a special friendship, neither did it mean a desperate search for a partner.

This is an area where many Christians have stumbled. Keep on praying, and remember that the Lord does truly understand.

▽ FURTHER STUDY QUESTIONS ▽

- How does Psalm 139 show that God is interested in us for who we are as unique individuals?

- In Genesis 2, was it singleness or loneliness that God saw as not being good? Is it fair to say singleness is our most natural state? How can singles overcome loneliness?

- Should we, like Adam, wait until God acknowledges our need and provides for it?

- In Matthew 19:10-12 and 1 Corinthians 7:25-40 how do Jesus and Paul refer to singleness as an acceptable, honourable and normal alternative way of life?

- Does 1 Corinthians 7:25-40 deal with dedicated Christian men writing to Paul asking if they were being unfair to the girls they loved by postponing marriage in order to devote their time and energy to the work of the Lord? Or what else is it saying?

- Make a list of single people in the Bible, and consider possible, positive factors.

- How can we let God use even the insensitivity of others to mould His character in our lives?

- Does Psalm 68:5,6 imply God's special help for single (solitary) people? How can marrieds and families offer support for those who are single?

- How can promises like that in Psalm 84:11 help us to avoid dwelling on negative emotions?

SUMMARY

FOR GROUP STUDY

SINGLENESS

* Singleness: our most basic state

* Coping with pressures

* A calling for some; a normal alternative

* A question of functioning as God intended

* Accepting the single state until God changes it

4.2 MARRIAGE

—duet or duel?

Main Bible Reading: Genesis 2:20-25; 1 Corinthians 7; Ephesians 5:22,23

There is a smart saying 'Marriage is not a word; it's a sentence!' Such a cynical view is, of course, a distortion of God's ideal. It was God Himself who officiated at the very first wedding, and ordained that marriage should be between one man and one woman, for life. It's not something to be taken lightly, or considered out-moded. In His teaching on the subject in Matthew 19:5, the Lord Jesus went back to the timeless principles of Genesis 2:24: '...*a man will leave his father and mother and be united to his wife, and they will become one flesh.*' Clearly, He saw the change in circumstances being a publicly witnessed occasion, requiring a permanent commitment, and finally to be consummated by the proper use of the gift of sexuality. The provision of a 'suitable helper' for Adam was to ensure companionship and mutual support, as well as providing for family development. From New Testament teaching the believer is to realise that the relationship between husband and wife is symbolic of that between Christ and His Church: '*For the husband is the head of the wife as Christ is the head of the church*' (Eph. 5:23).

What all this means is that the matter of choosing the partner with whom it is intended to share the rest of our life is a vitally important decision. The only person for whom a partner never had to be sought was Adam, because God provided Eve for him. Later, he described her as *'The woman...you [God] gave...me'* (Gen. 3:12, NKJV). As Christians, we will certainly want to seek God's guidance as to the partner He intends for us, although, unlike Adam, we have our part to play! God has already revealed key principles in His Word to guide us in this all-important matter. Let's look at Genesis 24 in which the Bible tells us quite explicitly how a wife was found for one of its great characters.

'Abraham was now old and well advanced in years... He said to the chief servant in his household... "...I want you to swear by the LORD,...that you will not get a wife for my son from the daughters of the Canaanites, among whom I am living, but will go to my country and my own relatives and get a wife for my son Isaac."

The servant asked him, "What if the woman is unwilling to come back with me to this land? Shall I then take your son back to the country you came from?"

"Make sure that you do not take my son back there," Abraham said. "The LORD, the God of heaven, who brought me out of my father's household and my native land and who spoke to me and promised me on oath, saying, 'To your offspring I will give this land'—he will send his angel before you so that you can get a wife for my son from there. If the woman is unwilling to come back with you, then you will be released from this oath of mine. Only do not take my son back there."...

Then the servant took ten of his master's camels and left, taking with him all kinds of good things from his master. He set out for Aram Naharaim and made his way to the town of Nahor. He made the camels kneel down near the well outside the town; it was towards evening, the time the women go out to draw water.

Then he prayed, "O LORD, God of my master Abraham, give me success today, and show kindness to my master Abraham. See, I am standing beside this spring, and the daughters of the townspeople are coming out to draw water. May it be that when I say to a girl, 'Please let down your jar that I may have a drink,' and she says, 'Drink, and I'll water your camels too'—let her be the one you have chosen for your servant Isaac..."

Before he had finished praying, Rebekah came out with her jar on her shoulder. She was the daughter of Bethuel son of Milcah, who was the wife of Abraham's brother Nahor. The girl was very beautiful, a virgin; no man had ever lain with her. She went down to the spring, filled her jar and came up again.

The servant hurried to meet her and said, "Please give me a little water from your jar."

"Drink, my lord," she said, and quickly lowered the jar to her hands and gave him a drink.

After she had given him a drink, she said, "I'll draw water for your camels too, until they have finished drinking." So she quickly emptied her jar into the trough, ran back to the well to draw more water, and drew enough for all his camels. Without saying a word, the man watched her closely to learn whether or not the LORD had made his journey successful.

When the camels had finished drinking, the man took out a gold nose ring...and two gold brace-lets... Then he asked, "Whose daughter are you?..."

She answered him, "I am the daughter of Beth-uel..."

Then the man bowed down and worshipped the LORD...and...went to the house, and the camels were unloaded... Then food was set before him, but he said, "I will not eat until I have told you what I have to say."

Finding a partner—lessons from Genesis 24

Abraham, the father, took the initiative in finding a partner for his son Isaac. In some parts of the world today it is still the custom to have 'arranged marriages'. These are not always to be deplored simply because it's not the custom in western society. The parents, or guardians, who arrange these marriages, being older and more mature, look for a partner whose lifestyle, and therefore expectations from marriage, would probably be identical to that of their children. Those who advocate the advantages of arranged marriages, will point out that marriages based entirely on feelings, although they may cross the barriers of wealth and upbringing, often come to grief over lack of finance, loss of status in society, or lack of ambition from one of the partners. In some lands, the 'dowry' system remains in operation, even in places where it is illegal. Money changes hands from the bride's family to the 'groom's and can be very belittling for the female. In a Hindu culture, for example, the teaching of 'karma' (fate) would help couples to accept each other and perhaps to work at their marriages more than in western culture. Should the question be asked, 'But do you love him?', the answer given may well be: 'I will learn to love him or her.' In some cases then, there may be very little freedom, if any, for the bride and bridegroom to put into practice the principles below. In others, Christian converts in such cultures may already have been ostracised by their parents and families, and, because of their conditioning, would tend to look to church elders to arrange partners for them. This might also happen when the parents themselves have been converted, although the couple themselves would expect some say.

Returning to Abraham, even though this was an arranged marriage, we still have to be impressed by the solemnity of his actions in calling for his chief servant and making him swear an oath that he'd do exactly as commanded, before entrusting him with the mission of finding a wife for his son. That just underlines the point we've made about the seriousness of this matter of finding a partner. We say again that it's not something to be taken lightly, as so often happens, sadly, in some societies.

Must I marry another believer?

We read of how Abraham on no account wanted his son's wife to be taken from the Canaanites, renowned as they were for their hideous pagan practices which were an offence to God. Even though Abraham's relatives, to whom the servant was directed, had become tainted with idolatry themselves, the knowledge of the true God had not died out completely among them. This condition reminds us of the New Testament commands to marry someone who '... *must belong to the Lord*' and not to be '... *yoked together with unbelievers*' (1 Cor. 7:39; 2 Cor. 6:14). Although the second verse is not dealing directly with marriage, we still cannot escape its implications for marriage, bound up as that decision is with our life of service for God. We're reminded of how, in Deuteronomy 22:10, the Israelites were commanded not to plough with an ox and donkey yoked together. An ox and donkey have different natures. This is also true of a believer and an unbeliever, and makes true partnership impossible. However openminded or sympathetic an unbeliever may seem, the fact remains that he or she is, by nature, hostile to God (Rom. 8:7). As a believer, how could you share your life with someone with whom you're not in agreement on such a profound issue—someone who doesn't share your love for the Lord Jesus? In that area you'd remain strangers. What about praying for their conversion? Sure, so long as your prayers aren't hindered by having already embarked on a course of action which is against God's will. Certainly never commit yourself emotionally before their conversion, for there are no guarantees, and there's always the danger of encouraging a false profession. Move in God's plan. If he or she really is 'the intended' then wait for their conversion—often this may indicate the Lord's will in terms of any future relationship. There may come a point, however, when you simply have to say that you can go no further. Other differences in background may be overcome with patience and understanding (e.g. the story of Boaz and Ruth in the book of Ruth).

A shared understanding of God's will

Abraham's servant then asks if he may take Isaac to Mesopotamia if the girl should wish to stay there. 'Absolutely not!', Abraham effectively replied. God had a special calling for Abraham and his descendents. He had promised the land of Canaan to them. There was to be no turning back.

In our case, it's vital that we find a partner who's prepared to follow with us in our calling, and share totally in our understanding of the Lord's will. Marriage for the Christian is to be '...*in the Lord*' (1 Cor. 7:39, NKJV). That will involve being subject to the Lord's will. The choice of a life-partner is to be governed by our allegiance to the Lord as well as by natural affection. This will mean that if we've come to a settled conviction about serving God in a way that is in accordance with Scripture and one which, as we see it, fully owns the Lordship of Christ, then we'll surely want to seek a partner who's not only a believer but who'll walk the same way and not take us to 'another land'. This is necessary in churches of God.

There's a very real practical difficulty in partners belonging to different denominations. Obviously, there's a limit to sharing, for example worship, which should be a shared highlight. And then, if there are children, whose way do they follow? At a very young age they'd be confronted with confusion and choices. A successful Christian marriage will depend on both partners fully agreeing in their desires for serving the

Lord. It's also important that our partner is prepared to support us in any special ministry for the Lord in which we are already engaged.

Seek God's leading

Abraham sends his servant off, assuring him that God will send His angel before him. That ought to impress on us that we, too, must trust that God will lead us in the matter of seeking a partner. The choice is of importance to Him. Traditionally, at least in western culture, it has been the male prerogative to take the active role in finding a partner. That left females with the more difficult passive role. Nowadays these roles have equalised somewhat, and young women who love the Lord would not be as hesitant as in generations past to make their feelings known, albeit discreetly, to the man of their choice. So, although the Bible story we're following is definitely from a male point of view, no bias is intended in applying its lessons today!

Look in the right place

The next thing that we find is that Abraham's servant took up a strategic position outside the city, by a well or spring. A friend of mine who was single once wryly remarked when reading through Genesis 24 that the first thing he thought he should do was to go look for a well! Joking aside, we can at least learn that although God may want us to have a partner, we must still do something ourselves! The servant didn't just sit in the desert and wait. We can go where we're likely to make friends with suitable potential partners. The servant went to a well. Water is often used in the Bible as a symbol of God's Word. We can make and deepen friendships at places and events where 'water is being drawn' in the study of God's Word—not that that should be our main reason for going there!

Pray

Notice how the servant next made it a matter of prayer that God would ensure that he met the intended woman. Nowadays, when the search for a partner is pursued by the young people themselves, we especially ought to pray for the Lord's leading. We need to begin to pray as soon as we feel the need for a life-partner, and definitely before we have someone special in mind. '...in all your ways acknowledge Him, and He will direct your paths' (Prov. 3:6 mgn). '...a prudent wife is from the LORD' (Prov. 19:14). No less can be said of a good husband.

Consider character

Pause next to observe the details of the servant's prayer. He didn't ask for the girl to be recognisable by what she wore, or by how attractive she looked; his request was more concerned with her character, shown by her willingness to do a considerable job of work! While physical attraction plays its part in a developing friendship, we see from this that it's not the prime consideration. A person's spirituality and character are more important grounds for compatibility than physical attractiveness.

Never be hasty

The servant waited until Rebecca had watered all the camels and he had talked with her. In that way he received complete assurance. How long should the period of going out and then engagement be? Certainly until you feel sure you really know the other person. By contrast there can be dangers in very long, as well as in very short courtships. There could be a sense of frustration, and the strain of maintaining purity could prove too much. Be sure to seek counsel from some wise, mature Christian couple well before the wedding day.

First get to know well

When at the girl's family home, the servant had to come directly to the point and fill the family in completely on the purpose of his mission. It's so important that would-be partners find out as much as possible about each other before any commitments are made. For example, it's vital to share attitudes and expectations about the question of starting a family. Such issues could be aired in pre-marriage counselling perhaps by the person invited to conduct the wedding service.

Working at marriage

Throughout a Christian marriage, the Lord should be regarded as a 'Third Partner' in the marriage. The spiritual aspect of married life is stressed in 1 Peter 3:7, which addresses Christian marrieds telling them that nothing should '...*hinder your prayers*'. Right from the start a daily pattern of sharing together in

Bible reading and prayer should be established, along with the practice of together bringing difficulties before the Lord as they arise from time to time. Proper biblical roles must be maintained (Eph. 5:23). The loving, self-giving headship of the man; the willing, God-honouring submission of the woman, as reflecting Godhead principles. This submission is as unto the Lord. If one partner has a difficulty in this the problem is, in reality, between them and the Lord. With each partner looking to Christ to meet their own basic needs (to be loved; to achieve; to feel valued), each must try to be a giver rather than a getter. The example of Christ's attitude to His Bride (the Church which is His Body) means there can be no self-assertion or domineering from the husband, but the highest respect for his partner's well-being in the authority relationship he bears to her.

A marriage—no matter how good—has to be worked at. This will often mean learning to be less selfish, being more sensitive to our partner's needs, and trying to continue to be as thoughtful for each other as in the days of courtship. Let's look at a few potential problem areas:

Communication

Lack of communication is a large factor in marriages foundering. Regular shared times of communication with God should be the basis for communicating in all other aspects of our lives. Listening is an important element of communication. True listening is not thinking about what you are going to say until after the other person has finished speaking! As well as talking, we need to share our feelings and aim at understanding. If a difference of opinion emerges, try to resolve it quickly (James 4:1-3; Eph. 4:26). The husband, as leader in the home, should take the initiative in seeking a solution. Views need to be aired (and feelings vented) in love (Eph. 4:15). It may be necessary to differ, but it will always be important to understand and, when appropriate, to forgive (Eph. 4:32).

Money

Financial stress is another potential hazard. A couple must learn to live within their budget. Keep accurate records of how you are spending your money. Be especially careful with credit cards. Remember the privilege and responsibility of giving to the Lord (1 Cor. 16:1,2).

Time

Make sure you agree on your principles of time management: time for God; for church activities; for being together; for overtime at work; for being (together/ separately) with friends. Discuss your priorities together. Beware of the danger of becoming over-committed to work or career, or any other thing that would cause your partner to feel neglected.

Sex

The Christian who is guided by the Word of God will have totally abstained from intercourse before marriage (see 7.1). Within marriage, God has designed that love be expressed through His gift of sexuality. Yet in a survey of Christian couples as to the sources of stress in their marriage, sexual relations ranked high on the list of answers close behind career, money and children. What was surely designed as the highest expression of intimacy within marriage can become, through misunderstandings and unfulfilled expectations, something of a strain on a marriage. Irregularity, for example, has its danger as 1 Corinthians 7:5 warns: *'Do not deprive each other except by mutual consent and for a time...so that Satan will not tempt you because of your lack of self-control'*. Be sensitive to each other's needs and wishes. The husband will understand that he is aroused and cools down more quickly than his wife. Psychologists make the generalisation that the female partner tends to be aroused by audible and tactile (touching) stimuli; whereas often the male partner reacts more to visual stimuli.

The Bible book of Proverbs (5:18,19) says *'May your fountain [your body parts which produce life] be blessed, and may you rejoice in the wife of your youth...may you ever be captivated by her love'*. Sex is the highest expression of love and intimacy in the marriage union. It's not only given to us for procreation. That brings us to conclude the section on the practical issue of family planning. Not everyone agrees with the practice or various methods of birth-control, so take advice and be informed before prayerfully exercising your personal conscience before the Lord in the matter (see 6.1).

▽ FURTHER STUDY QUESTIONS ▽

- What qualities would you look for in a partner? How many can be identified from Proverbs 31? What qualities should a husband express (see for example Ps.128)?

- Is it valid to think of God having a particular partner He intends for you?

- Is there a principle for us to apply from Amos 3:3?

- It was wrong for Israelites in the Old Testament to inter-marry with other nations. What parallel may be drawn from this today?

- What does being '...*joint heirs of the grace of life*' (1 Pet. 3:7 mgn) mean?

SUMMARY

FOR GROUP STUDY

MARRIAGE

* Finding a partner: lessons from Genesis 24
  — its seriousness
  — another believer
  — with a shared understanding of the Lord's will
  — seek God's leading
  — look in the right places
  — pray
  — consider character
  — never be hasty
  — get to know fully first

* Working at marriage: areas demanding attention
  — communication
  — money
  — time
  — sex

4.3 DIVORCE
—till death do us part?

Main Bible Reading: Matthew 19:3-9

'Some Pharisees came to him to test him. They asked, "Is it lawful for a man to divorce his wife for any and every reason?"

"Haven't you read," he replied, "that at the beginning the Creator 'made them male and female,' and said, 'For this reason a man will leave his father and mother and be united to his wife, and the two will become one flesh'? So they are no longer two, but one. Therefore what God has joined together, let man not separate."

"Why then," they asked, "did Moses command that a man give his wife a certificate of divorce and send her away?"

Jesus replied, "Moses permitted you to divorce your wives because your hearts were hard. But it was not this way from the beginning. I tell you that anyone who divorces his wife, except for marital unfaithfulness, and marries another woman commits adultery." '

Additional Readings: Deuteronomy 24:1-4

In some parts of the world as many as one in every three marriages ends in divorce. This leads to large numbers of children being emotionally disturbed, and this is just part of the terrible cost that is perhaps too little considered when marriages are terminated. In an age when Satan definitely seems to be attacking family life, what should be the Christian attitude to divorce? Many believers sincerely differ on aspects of this topic.

Since the Old Testament permitted divorce for a Jew on the ground of his having found '...*something indecent*' about his wife (Deut. 24:1), the Pharisees, in Matthew 19, asked the Lord Jesus for His attitude. They wondered whether He would be as lenient in His interpretation of the Deuteronomy law on divorce as some of the contemporary rabbis. They asked Jesus about divorce, but Jesus spoke to them about marriage, and about God's unchanging original ideal in marriage—one partner for life. He made it clear that only on account of the hardness of their hearts had divorce been tolerated as a concession within the Law of Moses. The Lord then went on to speak of adultery normally being involved when remarriage followed divorce (Mat. 19:9)—and that similarly anyone marrying a divorcee would be committing adultery (Mat. 5:32). In this way He endorsed most definitely God's original ideal from the time of Eden.

Making a judgement as to whether divorce would ever be tolerable, under any circumstance, involves coming to an understanding of certain difficult verses like Matthew 19:9. However, for the Christian who wishes to do the will of God, the Lord's words could not be plainer: '...*what God has joined together, let man not separate*' (Mat. 19:6). In Malachi 2:16 God says: '*I hate divorce*'. He could not have made more plain His attitude towards it. From the words of the Lord Jesus Himself, the Christian must accept that divorce is always wrong in the sense that it is a falling short of God's ideal in marriage. However, that is not to say that we should be anything other than sympathetic to anyone passing through the trauma of divorce, especially when they seem to be the victim.

In cases of severe marital difficulty, a period of separation is envisaged in 1 Corinthians 7:5, but with the aim of reconciliation. As Lawrence Crabb, a Christian psychologist states : 'If we deeply believe that the Lord is able to work for our good in all circumstances (Rom. 8:28), then no collection of marital setbacks will prompt us to seriously consider divorce.'

▽ FURTHER STUDY QUESTIONS ▽

- What does Jeremiah 3:1-8 tell us about God's own response to the unfaithfulness of His people?

- How are the principal different views of the 'excepting clause' in Matthew 19:9 explained?

- Comment on Jesus' words (John 4:18) to the woman He met at the well, a woman who had presumably been divorced five times.

SUMMARY

FOR GROUP STUDY

DIVORCE

* Divine institutions under attack

* An Old Testament concession

* God's attitude however: 'I hate divorce'

* Jesus reiterates the marriage ideal

* Divorce and remarriage normally involves adultery

* A solemn prohibition (Mat. 19:6)

* The alternative of 1 Corinthians 7:5 and Romans 8:28

FAMILY
ISSUES

5.1 THE FAMILY
—(i) a word to parents

Main Bible Reading: Deuteronomy 6:4-7

'The LORD our God, the LORD is one. Love the LORD your God with all your heart and with all your soul and with all your strength. These commandments that I give you today are to be upon your hearts. Impress them on your children. Talk about them when you sit at home and when you walk along the road, when you lie down and when you get up.'

Additional Readings: Psalm 27; Proverbs 24:3,4; Ephesians 6:1-4,10-18

The story is told of a relatively inexperienced speaker giving a talk entitled: 'How to raise your children'. Years later, he changed the title to: 'Feeble hints to fellow strugglers'! Recognising then the dangers of our own limited wisdom, let's stick as closely as possible to the God-given advice of our Deuteronomy reading. Here, through His servant Moses, God counsels His Old Testament people, Israel, how their families would be able to survive the many pressures they would be up against from the pagan society they would encounter in their new land. God's counsel is timeless, and especially relevant against the texture of today's largely post-Christian culture. Perhaps, there are four main things for parents to learn in looking at Deuteronomy 6:4-7:

Firstly, Deuteronomy 6:5 makes clear that their lives were to be permeated by a love for God. If God doesn't have first place in our lives, then our children will soon see that the spiritual things we offer to them are hypocrisy. Parents are to pass down to their children a healthy reverence for God, as well as an attentive ear to obey His voice.

Secondly, verse 6 made clear that God's truth had first to captivate their own heart. In the long run, it's what we *do*, more than what we *say*, that will shape the lives of our children. The effect of God's truth modelled in our lives should be to make our children 'thirsty for God'. Proverbs 22:6 is a great verse which says *'Train a child in the way he should go, and when he is old he will not turn from it.'* We should note that the word 'child' in the Old Testament is used to refer to anyone up to marriageable age, and the term 'old' here refers to maturity, not old age pensioners! Some translations make clear that the training is to be '... *according to his way'* (RV mgn); that is, each child is different, and in training each, we need to be sensitive to their God-given qualities. So we wouldn't necessarily bring up all our children in exactly the same way. Now, returning to our main point— the word 'train' comes from a word referring to the roof of the mouth, and was used to describe the action of a midwife dipping her fingers into the juice of crushed dates and then massaging a child's gums and palate. The tangy taste stimulated the child to suck. Spiritually then, in training children, the main object must be to stimulate their thirst for God and His truth. This will be impossible unless it first captivates our hearts.

Thirdly, verse 7 speaks about parents 'impressing', or 'teaching diligently', God's commands to their children. Literally, it might have been translated 'you shall intensely sharpen your children', which serves to show that such teaching that God has in mind is not passive, but active. The transfer of truth from one generation to the next is not automatic, but requires time and effort. The commitment to bringing up children to know and love and serve the Lord begins even before birth! Notice how in Judges 13 Manoah prayed '... *teach us how to bring up the boy who is to be born'* (v 8). Prayer is vital for our children lifelong.

Fourthly, the same verse goes on to speak about the need to talk about God's commands at all times in everyday situations. It's interesting that the Bible didn't use the Hebrew terms for 'preaching' or 'lecturing'. Using the word 'talk' shows that the transfer of truth is to be done naturally at all times. Above all else the home should be a place where God can be comfortably discussed in any conversation anywhere, but especially perhaps when the family sit down together regularly at meal times. It's a parent's natural desire to share things of real interest with their children —things like an interest in sport or wildlife say—but how much more important it is to teach our children about the Person who has transformed our lives. All this doesn't, of course, detract from the value and importance of having a daily family quiet time. As children see God's Word applied to everyday life, and family issues and problems worked through prayerfully, the mould will be set for their future lifestyle too. There are many useful publications available in Christian bookshops that help make family devotions exciting and enjoyable for all ages.

As we said at the beginning, it's easy for us to feel that parenting is such a daunting task that we don't have the necessary wisdom. But since our children are a trust from God (Ps. 127)—to be sent out like arrows to hit the mark in divine service—we can always come to God for help. What a wonderful resource we find in the book of Proverbs. Trace the more than 40 occurrences of the word 'son(s)', and share in the insights of the wisest father! It's a wise parent who understands a child's need for self-worth. Although the task is more difficult for some children than others, there are always ways of teaching a child his or her genuine significance, regardless of their physical appearance, or mental ability, or whatever. Every child needs to be secure in their parents' love and respect, which will lead to them accepting their own worth as a person. Every child has a right to loving communication and consistent discipline (Prov. 29:15) at all times, with violations of understood rules carefully explained—and the consequences!

▽ FURTHER STUDY QUESTIONS ▽

- Find at least five parental characteristics of Paul's nurturing of his spiritual children in 1 Thessalonians 2:8-12.

- Do you think Proverbs 22:6 gives us a guiding principle or a promise?

- What does biblical discipline involve? Consider the model given in God's dealings with His people.

SUMMARY

FOR GROUP STUDY

THE FAMILY (1)

* Four O.T. lessons for parents:
  — our lives to be permeated by love
  — God's truth to captivate our own hearts first
  — actively impress God's truth on our children
  — chat naturally about spiritual things at any time

* A child's needs and rights

5.2 THE FAMILY
—(ii) a word to sons and daughters

Main Bible Reading: Ephesians 6:1-3

> 'Children, obey your parents in the Lord, for this is right. "Honour your father and mother"—which is the first commandment with a promise—"that it may go well with you and that you may enjoy long life on the earth".'

Additional Readings: Mark 6:1-6; John 7:1-5

I hope that, if you have been brought up in a Christian home, you appreciate what a wonderful blessing that is, and all that really needs to be said is: *'Listen... to your father's instruction and do not forsake your mother's teaching'* (Prov. 1:8).

Inspired parental advice
We couldn't do any better than to receive the inspired parental advice of much of the book of Proverbs, covering as it does such areas as: standing up for our convictions (1:10-16); developing a relationship with God (3:11,12); coping with temptation (5:1-6; 23:19-21); managing our money (3:9,10; 6:6-8; 31:16;); the value of hard work (10:4,5; 13:4); our attitude to alcohol (23:26,29-35); and desirable qualities in women (31)! However, in our adolescent years, we often think we know better. Mark Twain expressed the sentiment

that it's about this time that we're amazed at how little our parents seem to know. Not long afterwards, we look back in greater amazement at how much they seemed to have learned in such a very short time!

Four common problems faced by four Bible young people

The teen years can be difficult as we struggle to come to terms with our own identity, demanding to be independent, yet also learning to take responsibility for our own actions, and deciding whose authority and values we're going to respect. The Bible gives us examples of teenagers and adolescents wrestling with these issues: there was Jephthah who was snubbed at home and so, in search of his identity, he got in with the wrong crowd (Judg. 11:1-3); Absalom who, exerting what he thought was his right to independent action, rebelled against the authority of a father who hadn't handled a family crisis firmly enough (2 Sam. 13-18); Josiah who, coping with early responsibility in his teens, looked to God for his values (2 Chron. 34:3); and Daniel who, like those today away from home to study, faced the alien pressures of life in a big city (Dan. 1) and showed respect for the God-given principles he'd been taught. It's true, of course, that as an exile and captive, he faced very severe constraints.

The example of the Lord

As a holy teenager the Lord Jesus Himself felt these same pressures (Heb. 4:15). Luke 2:52 says that Jesus grew in wisdom (mentally) and stature (physically), and in favour with God (spiritually) and men (socially). These are the four key areas of development in every adolescent's experience. How reassuring to realise that the Lord Jesus has been through it all, and left a victorious example for us.

Our reading in Ephesians also instructs us to follow the Lord's boyhood example of being subject, or obedient to His parents (Luke 2:51). What amazing humility and grace on His part, for there must have been times when He was right and they were wrong. But subjection isn't only for times when we can appreciate the other point of view. It is always, however, an opportunity to be Christlike (see also 1 Cor. 15:28). This passage in Ephesians is consistent with the Law of Moses, which also commanded respect for parents. And while fathers are not to exasperate their children, the children are to obey their parents in the Lord. This doesn't mean that there's no obligation to obey parents who aren't Christians. Rather, we're to obey our parents as we would obey the Lord Himself, for that's His will for us.

But perhaps our parents aren't Christians. We began this section by commenting on the real blessing of a Christian home where everything may be conducive to encouraging us to go on for the Lord. Your experience may, however, be different. Perhaps yours is a non-Christian, or divided home, and you find living the Christian life very difficult at home. I vividly remember listening once to some telling ministry on this subject developed from a delightful meditation on Jesus' own home life. The speaker felt that a window was opened on the Lord's own home circumstances when He said in Mark 6:4 'Only in his home town, *among his relatives and in his own house is a prophet without honour.'* This incident was the Lord's second rejection at Nazareth, where He had been brought up, and the sadness in His voice could almost be felt. Divisions in the home had cut Him keenly, and the hurts of some twenty-odd years surface in this remark. Young Christian, take heart, He Himself knows what it is to have a difficult daily life at home. And human nature being what it is, we can well imagine His half-brothers being resentful (see John 7) of their perfect older brother. So, if ours is a divided home, we can speak to Him about our problems, knowing He too has experienced them firsthand.

▽ FURTHER STUDY QUESTIONS ▽

- Look again at the parental advice given in Proverbs. Can you find anything that's out of date?

- What better options were open to Jephthah and Absalom?

- In what specific ways can we follow Josiah's and Daniel's lead?

- Which of the problem areas mentioned (identity, independence, responsibility and values) has been toughest for you?

- How does Jesus' example and experience help you?

- How can we contribute to good communication in the home?

SUMMARY

FOR GROUP STUDY

THE FAMILY (2)

* Inspired parental advice from Proverbs on:
  —standing up for your convictions
  —developing a relationship with God
  —coping with temptation
  —managing money
  —attitude to hard work
  —the dangers of strong drink
  —desirable qualities in women

* Four Bible teenagers and four common problems:
  —Jephthah: identity
  —Absalom: independence
  —Josiah: responsibility
  —Daniel: values

* The Lord's example:
  —as a holy teenager
  —as subject to His parents
  —as brought up in a divided home

MORAL ISSUES

6.1 CONTRACEPTION

—to use or not to use?

Main Bible Reading: 1 Corinthians 7:1-6

'Now for the matters you wrote about: It is good for a man not to marry. But since there is so much immorality, each man should have his own wife, and each woman her own husband. The husband should fulfil his marital duty to his wife, and likewise the wife to her husband. The wife's body does not belong to her alone but also to her husband. In the same way, the husband's body does not belong to him alone but also to his wife. Do not deprive each other except by mutual consent and for a time, so that you may devote yourselves to prayer. Then come together again so that Satan will not tempt you because of your lack of self-control. I say this as a concession, not as a command.'

Additional Readings: Genesis 1:28

The use of certain types of contraceptive is so widely publicised today that it may be thought almost unnecessary to question their use. As Christians, however, we must guard against the attitude of society around us causing us to lower our standards.

Let's be quite clear that we're talking here about their possible use within marriage by a Christian couple. Their use outside marriage to indulge in sex without unwanted pregnancies does absolutely nothing to change the nature of such sexual sin which the Bible prohibits (see 7.1). Intercourse between a man and a woman who are not married to each other is wrong whether 'protected' (so-called 'safe sex'; safe from the point of view of avoiding conception or disease) or not.

It has to be said that there are some Christians who see marriage, not to mention sex within marriage, as primarily, or only, for the purpose of obtaining children. They would therefore be content to leave the outcome of marital relations to the Lord, without taking any measures to prevent conception.

Yet the opening verses of 1 Corinthians 7 deal with the matter of voluntary restraint from sexual intercourse between husband and wife by common consent and seem to show that there is more to sex within marriage than simply obtaining children. Is it not also the highest expression of love, intimacy and union within marriage? Having said that, child-bearing is obviously prominently associated with it, and generally marriage is intended to bring with it the joys and responsibilities of parenthood. Some even see the concession of 1 Corinthians 7 as, in effect, justifying a natural means of contraception.

Some Christians, then, would feel at liberty to refrain from marital sex during the wife's monthly fertile periods. This is sometimes called the rhythm method of contraception. This could hardly be objected to biblically, if, out of a sense of the responsibility of providing adequately for them, Christian parents felt it desirable to limit and space their families. Family planning also allows young marrieds to enjoy togetherness first in preparation for starting a family later. It can also give a mother the opportunity to recover physically and emotionally between pregnancies. The method of withdrawal before emission by the male partner is sometimes regarded as another 'natural' method. It is, in fact, quite unnatural, can lead to frustration, and isn't recommended medically.

So, some other Christians, possibly concerned about the unreliability of the 'natural' methods, feel that there is no difference in principle between so-called 'natural' and 'artificial' methods. Examples of the latter type of contraception methods would be condoms and 'the pill'. However, the 'day-after' pill, which prevents fertilised eggs from implanting in the uterus, could be regarded as a form of abortion. The same would apply to some other methods, for example the use of intra-uterine devices. Since mechanical and chemical techniques are used to control our bodily functions in medical treatments, many see no real difference in this instance either. It's just yet another way of coming to terms with living in a now imperfect world. Perhaps, our main guiding principle should be that since our body is '... *a temple of the Holy Spirit*', and we have been '... *bought at a price*' (1 Cor. 6:19,20), any method shown to be harmful to the body should be avoided. In this, clearly, we may have to be guided by medical advice. The normally irreversible surgical treatment of sterilisation is probably best avoided except on health grounds.

A final thought: Christian couples who use 'artificial' birth control methods should be wary of selfishly avoiding the responsibility of parenthood, although it must be said that some reasons for having children could be just as selfish and irresponsible as other reasons for not having children.

▽ FURTHER STUDY QUESTIONS ▽

- What was wrong with what Onan did in Genesis 38:9?

- Is it more 'spiritual' to leave the outcome of marital relations to the Lord?

SUMMARY

FOR GROUP STUDY

CONTRACEPTION

* The purpose of sex

* Leaving the outcome to the Lord

* Special example of 1 Corinthians 7

* 'Natural' versus 'Artificial'

* Guidelines and dangers

6.2 INFERTILITY
—hopes unfulfilled

Main Bible Reading: Genesis 30:1-24

'When Rachel saw that she was not bearing Jacob any children, she became jealous of her sister. So she said to Jacob, "Give me children, or I'll die!"

Jacob became angry with her and said, "Am I in the place of God, who has kept you from having children?"

Then she said, "Here is Bilhah, my maidservant. Sleep with her so that she can bear children for me and that through her I too can build a family."

So she gave him her servant Bilhah as a wife. Jacob slept with her, and she became pregnant and bore him a son. Then Rachel said, "God has vindicated me; he has listened to my plea and given me a son." Because of this she named him Dan.

Rachel's servant Bilhah conceived again and bore Jacob a second son. Then Rachel said, "I have had a great struggle with my sister, and I have won." So she named him Naphtali.

When Leah saw that she had stopped having children, she took her maidservant Zilpah and gave her to Jacob as a wife. Leah's servant Zilpah bore Jacob a son. Then Leah said, "What good fortune!" So she named him Gad.

Leah's servant Zilpah bore Jacob a second

son. Then Leah said, "How happy I am! The women will call me happy." So she named him Asher.

During wheat harvest, Reuben went out into the fields and found some mandrake plants, which he brought to his mother Leah. Rachel said to Leah, "Please give me some of your son's mandrakes."

But she said to her, "Wasn't it enough that you took away my husband? Will you take my son's mandrakes too?"

"Very well," Rachel said, "he can sleep with you tonight in return for your son's mandrakes."

So when Jacob came in from the fields that evening, Leah went out to meet him. "You must sleep with me," she said. "I have hired you with my son's mandrakes." So he slept with her that night.

God listened to Leah, and she became pregnant and bore Jacob a fifth son. Then Leah said, "God has rewarded me for giving my maidservant to my husband." So she named him Issachar.

Leah conceived again and bore Jacob a sixth son. Then Leah said, "God has presented me with a precious gift. This time my husband will treat me with honour, because I have borne him six sons." So she named him Zebulun.

Some time later she gave birth to a daughter and named her Dinah.

Then God remembered Rachel; he listened to her and opened her womb. She became pregnant

> *and gave birth to a son and said, "God has taken*
> *away my disgrace." She named him Joseph, and*
> *said, "May the LORD add to me another son".'*

'Give me children, or I'll die!' was Rachel's sad cry one day (Gen. 30:1). That outburst seems to capture perfectly the pain and deep frustration felt by childless or infertile couples today. It reminds us of the intense suffering that results from infertility, particularly for the wife. It's too easy for those with families to dismiss the feelings of such couples, or to assume that they simply haven't planned to have children yet. It would be equally insensitive glibly to tell them simply to accept it as the Lord's will for them. Discovering the Lord's will must certainly be paramount, but the best thing we can do practically is to sympathise with them and, where appropriate, discuss compassionately the options of having children by means of adoption or modern medical technology. Counsellors would wish to underline the fact that it's our personal relationship with the Lord Jesus that should be our primary source of fulfilment. Reference has already been made in writing about 'Singleness' to our three basic needs of security, met by a love that we cannot lose; significance, assured by being gifted for a personal role in the Lord's service; and self-worth, realised by the value redemption puts upon us.

Advances in medical science are enabling people to live longer. Surgery and drug therapies have also improved the quality of life for many. It seems to follow then that medical science may equally well be used to overcome difficulties in the bodily function of producing life. Simple operations can often make it possible for people to produce children in the normal way. But what if this isn't possible? What further measures can reasonably be pursued?

Rachel's solution in Genesis 30:3 was to say to her husband, Jacob: *'Here is Bilhah, my maidservant. Sleep with her so that she can bear children for me and that through her I too can build a family.'* We might ask if we think she was justified in what she did, or did she go too far? Is the modern equivalent of this to use some versions of 'in vitro' (test-tube) fertilisation, artificial insemination, or surrogate motherhood?

We accept the use of artificial limbs, and artificial methods to carry out the function of our kidneys say, as well as artificial devices such as pacemakers to assist our hearts, so what then is the difference between these and artificial techniques to assist in the production of children? There would seem to be no difficulty in principle in accepting artificial means of placing the husband's sperm in his wife's body (artificial insemination by husband), or in bringing the husband's sperm and his wife's egg together in a test-tube (in vitro fertilisation by husband) before implanting in the wife's womb. Having said that, it is possible that specific procedures may offend the conscience of some because they involve masturbation (see 7.1) and foetal destruction. The latter may come about by 'spare' embryos, produced outside the body, being discarded after a successful implant. 'There are already 10,000 frozen embryos floating around in liquid-nitrogen baths in the US, stuck in a kind of icy limbo as their would-be parents sort out the options.'[1] Even greater controversy arises when such techniques use sperm that is not the husband's, or an egg that doesn't come from the wife. This would involve the introduction of a third party outside the marriage bond, and so its use must be rejected as not being permissible for the Christian.

---

[1] *'Cloning: where do we draw the line?'*, Philip Elmer-Dewitt, Time, Nov 8, 1992, p. 67.

▽ FURTHER STUDY QUESTIONS ▽

- How far should we go in not taking 'no' for an answer in infertility?

- How do we distinguish in practice between our own natural desires and the Lord's will for us? Need there be a conflict?

- Was Rachel's solution a satisfactory one?

- On what principles should we judge modern methods of overcoming infertility?

SUMMARY

FOR GROUP STUDY

INFERTILITY

* General usefulness of surgery and drugs

* Role of (all) artificial techniques

* Avoiding third parties

6.3 ABORTION

—a Christian's right to choose?

Main Bible Reading: Psalm 139:13-16

'For you created my inmost being; you knit me together in my mother's womb.

I praise you because I am fearfully and wonderfully made; your works are wonderful, I know that full well.

My frame was not hidden from you when I was made in the secret place.

When I was woven together in the depths of the earth, your eyes saw my unformed body.

All the days ordained for me were written in your book before one of them came to be.'

Additional Readings: Exodus 21:22; Psalm 51:5

In the first 25 years after the British Abortion Act came into force something like four million legal abortions were carried out in Britain alone. No wonder this consignment of unwanted foetuses to the hospital incinerator has been called 'The Silent Holocaust'.

The general debate is usually presented in terms of the rights of the mother versus the rights of the unborn child: that is the right to choose against the right to live. On the one side the talk is of retrospective contraception, on the other is the allegation of infanticide.

For the Christian, there can be no disputing the sanctity of human life. The command not to kill is clear. We may take animal life, but it's God's prerogative to take human life. The point at issue here is: 'when does human life begin?' Is it at conception, or when implantation in the womb lining occurs, or when brain function begins to be detected, or at the point when movement in the womb is first felt, or when the unborn child becomes capable of independent existence, or when the child draws its first breath, or at some other point?

Psalm 139, which stresses the embryonic development of the human body, suggests a sense of continuity from the time of conception. This encourages the utmost care for the well-being of the unborn child. David, in his famous confessional psalm, speaks of being '...*sinful from the time my mother conceived me*' (51:5). Taken at face value, this says clearly that our sinful nature derives from the time of conception. This is also true of our genetic identity. We are dealing with, at very least, a potential human life from the moment of conception—one which demands increasing respect as it develops towards the point where it is capable of independent existence.

Having said that, nowhere in the Old Testament is abortion explicitly condemned, although many other unethical practices are. Some versions read as though the penalty under the Law for causing a miscarriage (rather than a premature birth) was only a fine (Ex. 21:22). If that interpretation is correct, that might support the view justifying an abortion in certain circumstances. It could also be said that in miscarriages (the premature, accidental expulsion of a not yet viable foetus) we see 'natural' abortions taking place. This happens in as many as 12% of pregnancies, and many of these natural rejections have been shown to involve a potentially unhealthy foetus. This might suggest that it wouldn't necessarily be wrong to justify an abortion when the child-to-be was known to be severely handicapped. Of course, other Christian parents, after counselling, and after prayerfully seeking the Lord's leading, might well feel they would want to have such a child. Many can testify that their lives have been enriched, and God has been glorified, through caring for a handicapped child. Amniocentesis tests themselves, while carrying a slight risk to the developing child, are not always totally accurate in their predictions. That possibility would have to be borne in mind by parents, as well as recognising the guilt and depression that can be among the emotional side-effects of abortion. In cases where the mother is mentally handicapped, or under the age of consent, or a rape victim, those concerned would have to be guided by their personal conscience before the Lord wherever legal options existed, but it would be hoped that Christian friends would offer such support as to make a God-honouring choice possible.

In summary, it's not clear that the Bible completely prohibits termination of pregnancy. However, a Christian couple should only ever agree to an abortion when it is strongly advised on medical grounds, and after prayerfully seeking God's will.

▽ FURTHER STUDY QUESTIONS ▽

- Does Psalm 139 point to human life and personality in the womb?

- What do you think Exodus 21:22 is saying?

SUMMARY

FOR GROUP STUDY

ABORTION

* Exactly when does human life begin?

* A sense of continuity (Ps. 139)

* A biblical case for preferring the mother's life?

* An argument for induced miscarriages?

* No clear, complete biblical prohibition

* The guidance of personal conscience in special cases

* The underlying horror of millions of abortions 'on demand'

SEXUAL
ISSUES

7.1 SEXUAL STANDARDS
—who sets them?

Main Bible Reading: 1 Corinthians 6:18-20

> *'Flee from sexual immorality. All other sins a man commits are outside his body, but he who sins sexually sins against his own body. Do you not know that your body is a temple of the Holy Spirit, who is in you, whom you have received from God? You are not your own; you were bought at a price. Therefore honour God with your body.'*

Additional Readings: Genesis 2:20-25;
Proverbs 2:16-19; 5:15-20;
6:23-29; 7:6-27

'The Maker's operating instructions'

A traveller was one day honoured by being invited by the captain of the aircraft to come forward and inspect the flightdeck. Looking out into the great expanse of sky before him, he asked rather naively: 'Can you fly this plane anywhere you like?' 'Oh no', replied the pilot, 'we have to fly a course within an air corridor that's only 10 miles wide.' 'Don't you find that just a little restrictive?' 'No, because I know that to fly outside of that narrow corridor is to invite disaster...to be on a potential collision course with another aeroplane.'

The Bible introduces, celebrates and, at the same time, limits sex. Why does God limit it, we might ask? Well, as with all God's commands, this, too, is for our own good, and to defy our Maker's instructions is to court disaster.

But what about someone who might doubt that there's any valid reason for unmarried men and women not to have intercourse if they both wish to do so and have taken care to avoid the birth of an unwanted baby?

Let's be assured that God is far from being a kill-joy, and on this matter of human sexuality, as on all other subjects, the Bible makes very good sense when limiting sex to within marriage. Think of the unpredictable emotional effects of intercourse when performed outside of a successful marriage relationship. Moderate attraction may be changed by intercourse either into passionate commitment, or disgust. 2 Samuel 13:1-15 is an instructive example of this. Either way, people are likely to get hurt.

Promiscuity inevitably invites the drawing of comparisons between partners with all the potential for insecurity, hurt and rivalry that must bring. Advice that perhaps is more responsible sounding is that sexual experience should be confined to the context of couples who are committed to each other, or even more vaguely, who have a 'personal relationship'. If, however, the degree of commitment is total, why then should it not be expressed publicly, in marriage? The foundational trust of marriage itself can later be undermined by suspicions if the partners have indulged their sexual desires before getting married.

Sex is one of the biggest single issues facing young people today. Christian young people, who want God's best in their lives, will be guided by the Bible on this as on all other issues. The ancient advice given by father to son based on the wisdom of God in Proverbs 5:18,19 comes across today with just as much relevance: '*May your fountain* [your body parts which produce life] *be blessed, and may you rejoice in the wife of your youth... may you ever be captivated by her love*'. That sex is only intended as being between a man and a woman who are married to each other is clearly the Bible's message to us, as we shall see.

The problem, however, is that men and women are so easily drawn into wrong sexual experiences that are plainly selfish. Many simply cannot see the wood for the trees, or the love for the lust. It's tragic that it has to be the consequences of promiscuity that bring people to acknowledge the wisdom of following the Maker's instructions. A recent TIME magazine article spotlit the promiscuous sex indulged in by baseball and basketball athletes, and said that the possibility of contracting AIDS was now '... frightening enough to get some athletes thinking about the unthinkable: abstinence and marital fidelity.'

On the other hand, some people think self-gratification is all that is meant by sexual pleasure and, therefore, conclude that God never intended it for any other reason than procreation. However, the books of Proverbs, Song of Songs, and the early chapters of Genesis, teach us that God is not anti-sex, but has set His gift of sexual relations within the institution of marriage. This is for our own good and for our fullest enjoyment. As with many other things, something God created to be pure and beautiful, the highest expression of intimacy and union in marriage, has been distorted into something cheap and sordid.

Many in society today would say 'It's my body and I'll do what I want with it.' The believer on the Lord Jesus could never say that. For *'The body is not meant for sexual immorality, but for the Lord...Do you not know that your body is a temple of the Holy Spirit, who is in you, whom you have received from God? You are not your own; you were bought at a price. Therefore honour God with your body'* (1 Cor. 6:13,19,20).

Others in society appear to take a more responsible attitude in advocating 'safe sex', using the protection afforded by condoms etc. Such a view is often backed by government and medical authorities in an attempt to stem the tide of diseases like AIDS. This is presented as being more responsible, but, we must ask, is it any more biblical? No, for merely avoiding the consequences of our actions doesn't alter the fact one bit that sex outside of marriage is against God's will. Only sex within marriage is 'safe' from God's disapproval and judgement. God's standards are unchanging irrespective of changing attitudes in society. *'God will judge the adulterer and all the sexually immoral'* (Heb. 13:4).

How do I cope with sexual thoughts?

What about sexual desires?

First of all, it's normal to have these. God has created our sex drive, but we have the responsibility of making sure that we don't misuse it. It's not a sin to have sexual desires and to be tempted, but it is a sin to harbour them and give in to them in wrong actions. Someone has said that you can't stop birds flying over your head, but you can stop them nesting in your hair! We need to beware of fantasising, of entertaining ideas which aren't real and which may not be moral. In one of the old versions of Ezekiel (8:12 RV) we read about '. . . *chambers of imagery*'. Our minds can become 'chambers of imagery'. What pictures do we allow ourselves to drool over on the screen of our minds? There's the danger of allowing wrong thoughts to lodge in our minds, and to project pornographic images there. We're tempted sexually when pictures form in our minds, for example mental pictures of members of the opposite sex undressing. At this point we can resist them, or give in to them and let them have mastery over us—expressing themselves in such actions as masturbation (self-stimulation), or heavy petting.

By the way, there lies the problem in masturbation—namely what's happening in our minds. The Bible teaches that we, by the Holy Spirit's help, are to be masters of our thought life. As Paul exhorted, '. . . *whatever is true, whatever is noble, whatever is right, whatever is pure, whatever is lovely, whatever is admirable—if anything is excellent or praiseworthy—think about such things*' (Phil. 4:8). Try to use wrong thoughts as triggers to drive you into God's presence in prayer by cultivating such a reaction to these thoughts. In this way stumbling-blocks can become stepping-stones to God.

Often the best defence is to run (2 Tim. 2:22). If

we allow ourselves to watch every piece of garbage on TV, or look at suggestive pictures, then we shouldn't be surprised to find ourselves becoming sexually stirred. In the context of looking at a woman lustfully, the Lord said: *'If your right eye causes you to sin... throw it away'* (Mat. 5:29). In other words perhaps, don't look at what leads you to sin. Even if we are to be regarded as uncultured through not watching certain programmes etc, it will still be preferable to undergo such 'cultural amputation' by not allowing ourselves to watch them.

In the Bible, Job talked of having made a covenant with his eyes. Within a marriage, the attitude of adultery is condemned as well as the physical act (Mat. 5:28). Unfaithfulness begins by allowing ourselves to entertain romantic or sexual thoughts which don't include our partner.

None of us, however, is perfect, but when we become conscious of failure we should avail ourselves of the provision for forgiveness in 1 John 1:7-9.

How far should I go?

We've already mentioned petting and sexual arousal, another danger area when a couple are going out together. The Lord went on to say *'...if your right hand causes you to sin, cut it off and throw it away'* (Mat. 5:30). In other words don't do what leads to sin. Could we not apply this to petting? For our hands to sin could be for them to wander where they shouldn't. There are parts of each other's bodies that we shouldn't touch during the time we're 'going out'. To do so would be to allow ourselves to be aroused beyond control. A useful idea is to set agreed limits on exactly how far we go, and guard these limits for each other at all times.

A Swiss lady once advertised for a chauffeur and received three job applications. She interviewed them individually, each time asking the same question: 'How close to a precipice could you drive and still be safe?' The first assured her that he could come within 15 centimeters in complete safety. The second applicant boasted that he could let his outer wheel run on the edge and still have nothing to worry about. The third and last candidate admitted that he didn't know, but that he'd simply prefer to keep as far away as possible. Needless to say, he got the job!

Likewise, a couple going out together should steer well clear of going over the limits of control. For a couple to stop the car on the way home to say good-night and then to sit there for a very long time, is to invite temptation. Don't just share kisses and cuddles, but verses and prayers. Remember the spiritual dimension that's to be a key feature of any marriage (1 Pet. 3:7).

Going out with someone we consider to be a potential partner is a time for exploring each other's minds and hearts, not bodies. Perhaps, those too young to be even thinking of marriage should try to avoid 'pairing off' when developing special friendships. Such friendships will occur and can still be enjoyed in the company of others. Then, later, there may come a time when you decide to 'go out' with that person.

Even a couple who've been going out for some

time may say: 'We're not thinking of marriage just yet'. Fair enough, finding the right person—the partner of God's choice for you—will require getting to know them first as a friend. Spiritual qualities and personality are at least equally important dimensions as physical attraction, although the latter is usually why a relationship begins. Don't hurry, pray. God's timetable is perfect. Move in His plan, you'll not miss the boat. If you wouldn't even consider the person you're going out with as a person you might ultimately marry, then clearly your attraction is shallow, and your motives questionable.

Flirting is out for the Christian. It hurts people. It's certainly not God's will to play fast and loose with other people's emotions. However, flirting isn't simply how we behave, it may also be how we dress. '... *whatever you do, do it all for the glory of God'*. Do we dress to the glory of God (see 1 Tim. 2:9—'*modestly, with decency*'), or to be sexually attractive?

What about simply living together?

Finally, let's conclude by examining the Bible's message which, we've said, is to prohibit sex outside of marriage.

We've already quoted from 1 Corinthians 6 which condemns 'sexual immorality'. Someone, however, might ask: 'But how do we judge what is immoral—is it what society disapproves of?'

One genuine young couple with an eye on discipleship recently came to me seeking this confirmation: 'Please show us where the Bible teaches that two young people who love each other can't simply live together in a stable, loving relationship. What difference does a marriage certificate make anyway?'

Good questions! Certainly, in society generally, those couples enjoying a stable, loving relationship would feel more morally justified in having sexual relations with each other than those who casually engage in 'one night stands'.

The reasons advanced for couples preferring to live together as opposed to getting married might range from the economic advantages to the benefits of a trial period, or simply convenience of accommodation. However, the point is that in all these cases sex is placed outside of marriage.

When Jesus spoke to the woman by the well in John 4, He underscored the difference in status between her previous marriages and her then current state of living with someone. So, living together doesn't pass for marriage in the Lord's eyes. Fashion has no role to play in this, even if, as Christians, we have to swim against the stream (Ex. 23:2).

The only pattern for sexual relationships

Genesis 2:24 says: *'For this reason a man will leave his father and mother and be united to his wife, and they will become one flesh'*. Nowhere else does the Bible permit any variation of this practice.

Had God aroused Adam's need for a partner by bringing him into contact with the animals, each of whom had a mate? It was now clear to him that he had no 'suitable helper'. God, who had previously seen Adam's need for a partner before alerting him to it, then provided for that need to be met. From one of

Adam's ribs God made Eve, and gave her to him. In this way God officiated at the first marriage. Please note from verse 24 the three features of every marriage:

a) the loosening of former family ties. The man becomes head of his own family;

b) the forming of a new bond between the man and his wife. This is to be a permanent bond with one particular woman;

c) the physical union which symbolises and celebrates the marriage union as a whole.

It's vital to see that God's will only ever sees physical union, c), in the context of a) and b) above. And further, that these first two actions, a) and b), are actions that are to be witnessed.

A clear public act of leaving father and mother and becoming united to a wife is in view. The marriage itself isn't just a matter concerning only two people, it also has to do with society.

How that new bond between man and wife is made known is not the real issue (whether by means of a civil or religious service), but it should be publicly witnessed in some way. We reinforce this by saying again that the practice of cohabiting was not considered by the Lord as being, in effect, a marriage.

So, in all cases, sex outside of marriage is wrong—even after the point of engagement in a relationship that seems to be heading towards marriage. That sense of thrill and excitement is for after the wedding. If a young man and woman love each other very deeply, they'll show it by never asking one another to indulge in the sin of pre-marital sex. And, if they really do love each other, and are sure it is the Lord's will for them, then perhaps the time has come for them to think seriously about marriage (see 4.2).

Anyone who falls into the sin of pre-marital sex, or adultery, would lose their place of service in a church of God. However, as the extreme, and possibly habitual, case of 1 Corinthians 5:1-7 shows, the course of restoration remains open in all cases where true repentance is shown (2 Cor. 2:1-11). The example of king David's adultery shows not only God's forgiveness, but also the necessity of judgement still being carried out for the sake of maintaining a good witness, despite David's repentance (2 Sam. 12:13,14).

▽ FURTHER STUDY QUESTIONS ▽

- What reasons are given in 1 Corinthians 6 to show the seriousness of the wrong for the believer in practising sex outside of marriage?

- How does the language of Proverbs 2:12,16-19 compare with the media's glamorisation of prohibited sexual practices today? What is the effect of the latter on us?

- Can you recall an Old Testament story that vividly demonstrates the behaviour required by 2 Timothy 2:22?

- What lesson(s) may be learned from the record of Amnon's treatment of Tamar in 2 Samuel 13:1-15?

SUMMARY

FOR GROUP STUDY

SEXUAL STANDARDS

* Following our Maker's instructions

* Coping with sexual thoughts

* Determining how far to go

* Evaluating living together

* The only pattern for sexual relations

7.2 HOMOSEXUALITY
—an alternative lifestyle?

Main Bible Reading: Genesis 2:20b-25

'But for Adam no suitable helper was found. So the LORD God caused the man to fall into a deep sleep; and while he was sleeping, he took one of the man's ribs and closed up the place with flesh. Then the LORD God made a woman from the rib he had taken out of the man, and he brought her to the man.

The man said,

> *"This is now bone of my bones and flesh of my flesh; she shall be called 'woman,' for she was taken out of man."*

For this reason a man will leave his father and mother and be united to his wife, and they will become one flesh.

The man and his wife were both naked, and they felt no shame.'

Additional Readings: Genesis 19:1-13; Jude 7; Leviticus 18:22; 20:13; Romans 1:26,27; 1 Corinthians 6:9,10; 1 Timothy 1:8-11

Increasingly today we hear it asserted that sexual preference is simply a matter of taste. 'If a relationship is truly loving how can it be wrong?' is a question that's often asked. We hear believers and national church leaders openly acknowledge that they are 'gay'. Arguments are brought from the Bible to support these points of view. Can they be supported?

A crime or a sin—or both?

In some countries a homosexual act performed in private between consenting adults over a certain age is no longer considered to be a criminal offence. That's not to say that it's no longer to be regarded as immoral. There can be a big difference between what is legal in the eyes of men and what is right in the eyes of God. That difference is the difference between a crime and a sin.

Nature v. practice

The term 'homosexual', or 'gay'/'lesbian', can also imply different things. It can refer to what a person is by nature or to what a person is by practice. Certain studies have taught us to make a distinction between a homosexual orientation arising from environmental factors in childhood or possibly even biological factors with which a person may be born, and physical homosexual practices, for which those involved are, by contrast, most definitely responsible. Among homosexual relationships, there are those which are casual and those which claim to be stable, loving relationships.

What exactly is it that the Bible has to say on this subject?

Biblical prohibitions

There can really be no doubt that homosexual practices were among the sins of Sodom which attracted God's fearful judgement. In Genesis 19:5-9, Lot is asked by the men of Sodom to bring out his visitors *'that we may know them'* (RV), or *'so that we can have sex with them'* (NIV). It is the use of the word 'know' (Hebrew: yada) in the context of this passage which gives rise to the verse being understood as a request to have sexual relations with the visitors. The same word is used a few verses later to describe Lot's daughters who have never 'known' a man. This confirms the NIV translation as accurate. However, some may argue that this is only evidence against homosexual assault.

The best answer is to look elsewhere in the Bible. The prohibition *'Do not lie with a man as one lies with a woman; that is detestable'* (Lev. 18:22) is to be found in a general passage involving forbidden sexual relations, and is quite explicit against any homosexual physical practice. For all who take the Bible seriously, the clarity and force of this prohibition cannot be overstated. There is no limit as to whether only certain homosexual practices (e.g. gang rape, prostitution, shameless orgies, or corruption of the young) are taboo. Although there is undoubtedly a religious context to this prohibition (see e.g. vv 19,21), it cannot be argued that the ban does not extend to homosexual behaviour without religious overtones, because incest and adultery are also condemned. We must see Leviticus 18:22 as an unequivocal statement covering every form of homosexual practice, confirmed by the writings of

Paul listed above. The most common word used by Paul (Greek: arsenokoites) covers all homosexual behaviour and not only those who have personally abandoned heterosexual practice. In Romans 1:18-32, homosexuality is seen as a sign of people's rebellion against God, although not the only one. Both homosexual behaviour and the condoning of such practices are condemned.

On the other hand, if someone claims to have a homosexual orientation, then it is our duty to support them in what will have to be for them a celibate lifestyle, at least as far as relationships with the same sex are concerned. Loneliness could be a real problem. We should aim at understanding, not prejudice. Christians with a homosexual orientation have testified to the overcoming grace of God in living with this human weakness, when a changed pattern of sexual desires, although prayed for, has not apparently been granted. The power to control our strongest urges (and our sex drive is one of them) is part of the fruit which the Holy Spirit produces in a yielded believer's life (Gal. 5:22,23). 1 Corinthians 6:9-11 demonstrates it.

The seal of Genesis 2

In case there should be any lingering doubt as to whether there could ever be a biblically acceptable alternative to a heterosexual marriage relationship (after all, we live in the days of the so-called 'Gay Christian Movement' and when the validity of 'gay' clergy is increasingly acknowledged in some established churches), let's remind ourselves of the original, divine institution of sex and marriage in the Bible record of creation. Genesis 2:24 states: *'For this reason a man will leave his father and mother and be united to his wife, and they will become one flesh.'* God's design for human family units is for the union of one man and one woman ('a man', 'his wife'). This union is to be publicly recognised ('leave his father and mother'—a public social occasion is in view), next it is to be permanently sealed ('be united to'), and finally it is to be physically consummated ('one flesh'). The Bible does not envisage any other kind of marriage or place for sexual relations; God has not provided any alternative.

For those who do practise physical homosexual activity, 1 Corinthians 6:9,10 makes clear that they can have no part in God's kingdom. Therefore, they could not continue to have a place of service in a local church of God.

Maybe we should mention here that whereas AIDS once appeared to be a disease specifically relating to homosexuals, this is no longer the case. The first wave of media attention targetted homosexuals, the second wave drug-users, and the third wave heterosexuals. While in Europe and North America the disease spreads mainly by homosexual transmission; the spread is mainly by heterosexual transmission in Sub-Saharan Africa, Asia, Latin America and the Caribbean. In Africa, it is a family disease since in many areas polygamy is still the norm. This has led to large numbers of babies also carrying the infection. Thirty percent of women with AIDS were virgins when they married and have been faithful wives.

Of course, all along there have been those, tragically, who have been infected quite innocently (e.g. when receiving health-care). When the disease does arise out of deviant sexual practices it can only be viewed as a consequence of such (Prov. 6:27,28; Rom. 1:27), and compassion shown to the victims.

▽ FURTHER STUDY QUESTIONS ▽

- Are there any reasons why Leviticus 18:22 should not apply today?

- How can we love the sinner and yet hate the sin?

- How can we best support those requiring to remain celibate?

SUMMARY

FOR GROUP STUDY

HOMOSEXUALITY

* 'Crime' as opposed to 'Sin'

* 'By Nature' as opposed to 'By Practice'

* Old Testament prohibitions
  corroborated in the New

* The seal of Genesis 2

IN CONCLUSION

In the sixteenth century the Reformers placed great emphasis on 'sola scriptura' (Scripture alone for our authority). If you've read through some or all of the issues that this book treats you'll have noticed that here, too, the final court of appeal is the Word of God, the Bible. This is because we believe the Bible to be the sole authority for the Christian faith. In Jude 3 we read that the faith (meaning here the body of Christian teaching) was '...*once for all entrusted to the saints.*' The same expression is used in Hebrews (e.g. 10:10) to describe the finality of Jesus' sacrifice on the cross. Equally then, the doctrines of the Christian faith, delivered to us in the New Testament by the apostles and prophets, are God's final word to us. As Jesus' finished work alone is sufficient to save us, so the inspired Word is sufficient to guide us on all issues affecting our lives and service for the Lord.

The Lord Jesus taught that if we love Him, we'll obey His Word (John 14:15). Legalism isn't the answer, but love to Christ is. How then may our love to Christ be encouraged? In human experience we find, do we not, that love between two people grows as they spend time in one another's company, as they gradually get to know each other better, and come more and more to appreciate qualities in each other that are suited to their needs and temperaments. As we become more familiar with our Bible, we become more aware of just how much the Lord Jesus cares for us, and we find our heart being drawn out to Him in response. We discover that His qualities are precisely suited to our needs (see Heb. 7:26). Just as a young couple who are in love set times for seeing each other, we too need to set aside time for spending in the company of the Lord, to enjoy communion and fellowship with Him around His Word. It was talking with Him about things concerning Him in the Scriptures that caused the two disciples to have that heart-warming experience of fellowship en route to Emmaus in Luke 24. He drew near to them without revealing Himself physically to them in a recognisable form. Similarly, today, we don't know His physical presence but spiritually He seems to draw near as the Holy Spirit reveals Him to us in the Bible portion we're meditating upon. Meditation in this sense is talking to the Lord about Himself and ourselves. As the love of our hearts for Him is kept warm in this way by spending time in His company, and so growing in our knowledge of Him, so more and more we'll want to do the things He asks of us in His Word, for He says in John 14:15 that if we love Him we'll keep His commandments. Whenever we feel our love waning, for in all our cases it still ebbs and flows, we can always make it our prayer that we might be granted the capacity to love Him more, always confessing any failure or neglect on our part. As well as systematic Bible study it's a good idea to have a separate scheme of devotional reading time. When we're motivated by the desire for His fellowship such times will be no mere duty for us, will they?

The Psalmist said: *'I have hidden your word in my heart that I might not sin against you'* (119:11). The original word 'hidden' is the same as when Moses' mother 'hid' him for the first three months of his life. If we take the same care to hide God's Word in our heart as that mother did to protect the precious cargo of her darling infant, then we'll be able by God's help to guard our heart from which come 'the issues of life.'

BIBLIOGRAPHY

The following books are recommended for further reading around the subject matter presented in this book. This is not meant to endorse all that is contained in these books, but to suggest that they are worthy of study by the discerning reader. I have found them helpful.

Issues facing Christians today (Marshalls) by John Stott 1984

In His Image In His World (CWR) edited by Eddie Tait 1990

Boy/Girl Relationships (Torbay) by Simon Matthews (1976) 1987

Eros Defiled (IVP) by John White (1977) 1986

Homosexuality: what does the Bible say? (UCCF) by David Field 1988

The Challenge of Singleness (Marshalls) by Trevor Partridge 1982

Ten Principles for a Happy Marriage (Marshalls) by Selwyn Hughes 1982

Family Planning (Triangle) by Gail Lawther 1985

Growing Wise in Family Life (IFL) by Charles Swindoll 1988

The New Age Movement (CMS) by Paul Young 1991

Celebration of Discipline (Hodder) by Richard Foster (1989) 1990

PERSONAL STUDY NOTES